10 Steps to Develop Great Learners

What can concerned parents and carers do to ensure their children, of all ages, develop great learning habits which will help them achieve their maximum at school and in life? This is probably one of the most important questions any parent can ask and now John Hattie, one of the most respected and renowned Education researchers in the world draws on his globally famous Visible Learning research to provide some answers.

Writing this book with his own son Kyle, himself a respected teacher, the Hatties offer a 10-step plan to nurturing curiosity and intellectual ambition and providing a home environment that encourages and values learning. These simple steps based on the strongest of research evidence and packed full of practical advice can be followed by any parent or carer to support and enhance learning and maximize the potential of their children. Areas covered include:

- Communicating effectively with teachers
- Being the 'first learner' and demonstrating openness to new ideas and thinking
- Choosing the right school for your child
- Promoting the 'language of learning'
- Having appropriately high expectations and understanding the power of feedback

Anyone concerned about the education and development of our children should read this book. For parents it is an essential guide that could make a vital difference to your child's life. For schools, school leaders and education authorities, this is a book you should be encouraging every parent to read to support learning and maximize opportunities for all.

John Hattie is Emeritus Laureate Professor at the Graduate School of Education, University of Melbourne, Australia. He is one of the world's best-known and most widely read education experts and his Visible Learning series of books have been translated into 29 different languages and have sold over 1 million copies.

Kyle Hattie is a Year 6 teacher working in a primary school in the northern suburbs of Melbourne, Australia. Over his 10-year career, he has taught at many year levels, from Prep to Year 6 in both Australia and New Zealand. Kyle has held various leadership titles and has a passion for understanding how students become learners.

"John Hattie has devoted his life to helping children learn—and enjoy learning. This book is chock full of great ideas for how parents can help their children become eager and effective learners."

Carol Dweck, author of 'Mindset' and Lewis & Virginia Eaton
Professor of Psychology, Stanford University, US

"A provocative new look at how parents can best support their children's learning underpinned by both in depth research evidence and hands on parenting. From the man who used mass research to show teachers how to get the best out of their teaching and his school-teacher son, an irresistible combination and a fascinating insight for parents."

Wendy Berliner, author of *Great Minds and How to
Grow Them and How to Succeed at School*

"The most precious gift we can give our children is the confidence, capacity and appetite for learning. To not shy away from things that are challenging, changing and complicated is the foundation for a fulfilling and adventurous life. But how best to lay that foundation? In their new book, father and son team John and Kyle Hattie offer sound, practical advice that is based on an irresistible blend of solid scholarship and wise first-hand experience. One of the best parenting books I have ever read."

Guy Claxton, author of *The Learning Power Approach*
and *The Future of Teaching*

"As a father of three and an educationalist, I have read many books on family education. When I got John and Kyle Hattie's manuscript to read, something happened that has never happened before: I couldn't stop reading! From my point of view, the book is a treasure trove of helpful hints and vivid examples, full of life experience and scientific foundation. The latter is worth emphasising from my point of view: everything that is presented in the book can be scientifically proven - and that without having a scientific duct. In my opinion, this makes the book stand out in the long line of parenting guides that often spread more myths than truths. In other words, it is a book in which research and practice merge and parents get the help they need to give their children the best possible education."

Klaus Zierer, Professor of Education,
University of Augsburg, Germany

Praise received for John Hattie's previous work:

"Reveals teaching's 'holy grail'"
Times Educational Supplement

"John Hattie has made a supersized contribution to the improvement of learning. Visible Learning came crashing on the scene in 2009 and got the attention of all of us. What I especially like is how Hattie and team continue to be internally critical and externally open to considering all possibilities. Their new series in search of 'the Gold Standard' is typical of Hattie's commitment and skill in processing criticism and modelling continuous learning and improvement. A million books! Congratulations for a monumental achievement and the promise of more, and more"
Michael Fullan, OC. Professor Emeritus,
OISE/University of Toronto

"I'm not sure John knows his own impact - I can't think of anyone in education on this planet with a higher effect size. We teachers needed a sieve to sort the research that helps teachers make a difference, from the research that doesn't. John provided it and now we all know how to increase our own impact. Thank you John!"
Geoff Petty, Author of 'Teaching Today' and
'Evidence-Based Teaching'

"Education research suffers from an embarrassment of riches— there's too much of it! John Hattie has been a resolute leader in summarizing this wealth of information into practical terms that are digestible yet reliably capture the essence. Better still, they translate readily to classroom practice! Hattie's success and influence are richly deserved."
Dan Willingham, Professor of Psychology, University of West
Virginia, author of 'Why Don't Students Like School?'

"Everything changed when Visible Learning revealed the key messages from research into influences on learning. Thousands of studies brought together confirmed what we must focus on ... educators across the world continue to have a reference point for what matters in guiding thinking and practice."
Shirley Clarke, Author of 'Unlocking Formative Assessment'
and 'Thinking Classrooms'

"John Hattie's contributions to generations of students, teachers, and educational leaders around the world are profound and lasting. He has that rare combination of courage and humility, fearlessly challenging conventional wisdom while continually improving and expanding his work. He makes our profession and the world of education better, and children on every continent benefit from his scholarship, wisdom, and practical guidance."

Douglas Reeves, Creative Leadership.net

"Hattie's work enables us to see the effects of what teachers do in the classroom. His work on lesson preparation is one of those must-reads for all teachers. In teaching we are often looking for those light-bulb moments of illumination. Hattie has mapped the hidden wiring."

Huw Thomas, Former Headteacher, college lecturer
and Diocesan Director of Education

"In a world where educators are often tempted and encouraged to utilize the latest fads to support student learning, John Hattie's Visible Learning books serve as exceptional resources. Every practicing teacher, school administrator, and education researcher should have these books on their shelves."

Eric M. Anderman, Professor of Educational Psychology,
The Ohio State University

"John Hattie has a dream that one day every child learns not by chance, but by design. He has a dream that one day the expertise which is all around us gets together and changes the system. He has a dream that one day teachers ask themselves the powerful question "What works best?" instead of only "What works". And he has a dream that one day teachers always seek maximum impact. And – most important – he lives his dream. He has started the fire with his passion. He sparked the learning. And he sparked the teaching. Congratulations John and: Know your impact!"

Klaus Zierer, Professor of Education, University of Augsburg,
Germany, and Associate Research Fellow of the ESRC-funded
Centre on Skills, Knowledge and Organisational Performance
(SKOPE) at the University of Oxford

10 Steps to Develop Great Learners

Visible Learning for Parents

John Hattie and Kyle Hattie

 Routledge

Taylor & Francis Group

LONDON AND NEW YORK

Cover image: © Getty Images

First published 2022
by Routledge
4 Park Square, Milton Park, Abingdon, Oxon OX14 4RN

and by Routledge
605 Third Avenue, New York, NY 10158

Routledge is an imprint of the Taylor & Francis Group, an informa business

British Library Cataloguing-in-Publication Data
A catalogue record for this book is available from the British Library

Library of Congress Cataloging-in-Publication Data
A catalog record for this book has been requested

ISBN: 978-1-032-18928-4 (hbk)
ISBN: 978-1-032-18929-1 (pbk)
ISBN: 978-1-003-25702-8 (ebk)

DOI: 10.4324/9781003257028

Typeset in Bembo and Helvetica Neue
by Apex CoVantage, LLC

Contents

Preface

One of the best things we ever did – have children. Gone were the fun nights, gone were the flash cars and in came the SUVs, four suitcases for them and a backpack for us, the you that you knew disappeared and a new persona developed.

The older one of us has been blessed with three children and five grand children, and the younger has two of these grand daughters. While we learned lots of parenting lessons over the years, the most important lesson was to never criticize other people's children or make negative comments about other parents. Our parenting is far from perfect. Even with many decades of education research and teaching between us, we know from first hand experience that parenting is hard and unpredictable. At times it is glorious and at times almost unbearable.

Like all families, we have many stories, and throughout this book we tell tales. In most you can guess where the perspective is Kyle or John, but it does not matter too much. Our children are no angels. Like every parent, we wanted to believe that every time our children messed up it was their doing, and every time they were perfect it was our doing. When our sons won gold medals at world games, it was obviously due to genetic influences. At times we glossed over our parenting errors and took undue credit, but of course, we know that is not how it works.

Most important of all, we had fun being with our kids as they grew up, and like most parents since the dawn of time we learned our parenting skills 'on the job' mostly by trial and error. We have lived in six countries, our children have attended school in four countries, and we have moved as a family to a new house over 30 times. Our children have truly experienced the world in a way the older one of us would never have imagined when he grew up in rural New Zealand (the country did not have television until he was 16, he never traveled more than 30k from home until 16, and there was a blessed naivety of growing up in a rural town). Despite all this and the errors we made, our children turned out to be fine adults.

In the past decades, the involvement of other adults in children's lives has greatly expanded. This book is not just for parents but rather for all people in a child's life who are involved in their parenting. More and more, the people undertaking the parenting role are likely to be grandparents, older siblings, foster parents, two dads or two moms, and so many other permutations. One of the many beauties of New Zealand is that there is a rich Māori parenting tradition of whānau, which is more than just direct family. It encompasses values, histories, and traditions from the ancestors and community in which a child belongs. It relates to how a child understands their broader relations both past and present, the child's sense of personal spirituality and inner self, and teaching a child their deeper responsibility to the community and traditions.

Children are becoming less 'owned' within a single traditional family unit but owned and influenced by so many outside that unit. Whānau is a wonderful concept and creates the sense of 'village': a child is brought up within a whānau. Well, sometimes, but too many now are enveloping their children, and overprotecting them from risks and the 'unknown'. No longer do we let children roam the village, call them in for meals, and presume they are safe – ironically, it is in the safest neighborhoods where too many parents are most worried about safety. There is a balance between concern for safety and learning boundaries. We refer to this as parents developing the dignity of risk in their whānau.

The learning lives of children

This book aims to highlight the balance, learning the dignity of risks and the boundaries, and it focuses on the 'learning lives' of children by explaining what you can do to promote learning, the role of parents in schools, and how to be your children's center of experiences, love, and teachings.

We are not supportive, however, of the notion that parents are a child's 'first teacher' – as this too often confuses the role of parent and school teacher. We argue that the role of parents is to be parents first and always be the 'first learner', demonstrating and being open to learning, talking the language of learning, and instilling the skills and thrills of learning with their children. We leave to teachers to teach the schoolwork, to develop skills of learning schoolwork, but of course, the boundaries are blurred. As you will see, we expect much from teachers and will show how you can complement making your child a great learner.

This is not a book about how to make better parents in terms of behavior, physical health, or health issues – which are of course part of your critical role. There are already so many resources for these roles. Instead, our focus is on learning and the role that every parent can and should play in their child's learning – at home and while they are at school.

The book is structured around 10 major mind frames. These mind frames focus on ways of thinking about parenting – as it is the thinking, the decisions, the interpretations that we make about our children that matter most. Two parents can 'do' the same thing, but the intention, the thinking, the mind frame behind this thinking, is what matters most and makes the difference. Clarity between what we think and what we do can be a major source of friction in families, particularly for children who may not be as adept at understanding and interpreting what you mean. As I said to my sons many times – do what I mean, not necessarily what I say (perhaps cruel and unusual punishment).

In other books, we have developed mind frames for teachers and school leaders, and we are working on one for students. A mind frame is a way of thinking, a set of beliefs, skills, and feelings that guide talk, actions, and decisions. The more explicit we can be regarding these mind frames, the more successful our children are in interpreting what we mean.

It's no surprise that we form strong reactions to how we were parented or cared for based on our own experiences and vow to 'never do that to our own children'. JH was brought up in the 1950s. It was still expected that children were 'seen and not heard'. The strap and smacking were the norms, the town was small, and the horizons even smaller. The aim was to enjoy the 'now' as the future was ordained somehow, somewhere else, and later. KH was brought up in the '90s in the US when the world was getting smaller and the options for work, socializing, and travel started to explode. So too did the expectations become better and brighter, and children were to be 'seen and heard'.

You know more than you think you do

The eldest (JH) started thinking about his role as a parent during his university studies in child development at the University of Otago in Dunedin. One snowy and very cold Dunedin Sunday, he walked many miles to the town hall for a special lecture by Dr Benjamin Spock. Spock was a world-famous pediatrician who wrote the all-time best seller – *Baby and Child Care* that encouraged parents to see their children as individuals rather than seeing the role of parenting as rule keepers or being obliged to follow a one-size-fits-all approach to parenting.

Spock promoted the idea that parents should 'trust their instincts' and began his book 'You know more than you think you do'. He noted that routines are nice but regimes are not. He argued that there is no need for strict, regular feeding or sleeping schedules. Spock included advice for mothers and even for fathers – and it was very novel at the time to mention fathers in child rearing books. He fought against childhood obesity and welcomed gay and lesbian parents. It may seem absurd today, but his most powerful message was that 'babies need love' and that cuddles, hugs, and kisses do not spoil your child. His central message was 'while you are trusting yourself as a parent, remember also to trust your child'.

Not everyone liked Spock's advice. In the 1970s, Norman Vincent Peale (a famous US minister and author) claimed that 'the U.S. was paying the price of two generations that followed the Dr Spock baby plan of instant gratification of needs'. Peale argued that this led to disorderliness, permissiveness, and adolescent misfits protesting the US involvement in Vietnam. While this is a major misinterpretation and overreaction to Spock's advice and influence, he was actually an outspoken critic of US involvement in Vietnam – and Vietnam was what he had come to our town hall to talk about.

The problem, on the snowy Dunedin Sunday, was that when JH arrived there was no one else there. The talk had been postponed for four hours because of a bad snowstorm and I must have been the only person not to hear this announcement. So what to do – walk home or wait the four hours till the new time. So I sat on the front step of the town hall and waited. Soon after, Dr Spock arrived (lucky for me he too did not hear the postponement message), and so he asked if I could help him distribute his flyers onto the empty seats in the hall. Three hours of wonderful conversation later, we become best friends for the afternoon.

I regret now never thanking him for influencing my parents and millions of others 'to give me space, freedoms, love and trust' (and I also never told him that I was really there that afternoon to see the childcare expert, not the Vietnam War campaigner). Unlike the other Mr Spock, he encouraged the expression of emotions and having fun whilst still a child. I am forever grateful that he did not prescribe fixed parenting regimes or encourage parents to keep their distance, and he fought against the idea that children should be 'seen and not heard'. He popularized the idea that we now take for granted – that children are entitled to live, grow, and be happy and challenged. My parents were Spoke-ites, and I am all the better for it.

The unrelenting focus in the book is on the role of parents to develop 'open-to-learning' children – by doing this themselves, not only by being curious, failing often and learning from this failure, being responsive, and being a great listener but also by being the moral compass in the center of this learning and its outcomes.

Acknowledgments

JH's parents, Jack and Molly, created a loving environment for their four kids to grow and thrive. Dad was a cobbler when I was born and then joined the tax department, and Mum was a 'housewife', then managed a movie theatre, and owned a knitting shop. KH's parents, Janet and John, were teachers and academics, creating a home of fun, learning, and exploration. They spent lots of time supporting us with learning and teaching us to explore our surroundings. With many moves in house and country (30 different houses in four countries) we learned from a young age to embrace change and become resilient. They moved us around the world a lot.

Janet and John had three boys, and now five granddaughters, and are reliving parenting with all fun and no responsibility (we are the 'naughty' grandparents). So much of this book comes from lessons we have learned as parents and from our parents. Yes, we have read so many parenting books, academic articles on parenting, and conducted our own mini-synthesis of the meta-analyses on parenting. Thanks to all involved in the Hattie whānau.

As an adult KH is constantly reading and learning about his craft as a teacher and an aspiring academic. He is supported by his wife, Jess, also a teacher, and his two beautiful children, Emma and Danielle. His family is his inspiration for all his learning and everything he does. Ditto for JH – Janet is his love, best critic, fun to be with, and I learned so much about parenting from her parenting of our kids (and of me). We also thank Joel, Kat, Ella, Florence and Indy, Kieran, Aleisha, Riley, Kobi, Edna, Patterson, Thompson, and Henry as they are core members of the Hattie whānau.

Ruth Aston (who made the difference to the Appendix), Jason Manning, Tom Davies, Klaus Zeirer, Adrian Piccoli, Marilyn Fleer, and a particular thanks to Janet Rivers – not just an editor but also a designer, creator, and enhancer. Bruce Roberts from Routledge again oversaw the project, showed remarkable patience with the slowest authors (it took six years to write this book), and harnessed the reviews, production, and Routledge commitment to producing the best possible book.

Preface

The purpose of this book is to explain how parents can better support and promote their children's learning. It is not a book about how to make better parents in terms of children's behavior or physical health or other such critical parts of the parenting role. There are already many resources for those aspects. Our focus is solely on learning and the role that every parent can and should play in their child's learning, both at home and at school.

We argue the role of parents is to be parents first and to always be the 'first learner', demonstrating and being open to learning, promoting the 'language of learning' (i.e., discussing learning and developing a culture of learning), and instilling the skills and thrills of learning with their children. We do not promote the notion of parents as a child's 'first teacher', as this would confuse the role of parent and school teacher. We leave it to the teachers to teach the schoolwork. What we show you is how you can help make your child a great learner.

We use the terms *parents* and *parenting* in the widest possible sense. This is a book for all people involved in the child's upbringing, be they mother, father, grandparents, older siblings, foster parents, families of two dads or two moms or an extended family, and all other permutations of parenting.

Parenting mind frames for children's learning

Each chapter in this book is centered on a parent mind frame (describing the attitudes and attributes required for each 'step' on the journey to creating a great learner) to guide parents thinking about how to support their child to become the best learner possible. A mind frame is a way of thinking, a set of beliefs, skills, and feelings that guide talk, actions, and decisions. In our other books, we have developed mind frames for teachers and school leaders, and we are working on one for students.

Let children live, enjoy, and discover as children

An important message in this book is that children are not there to be developed for some future time; they need to enjoy being children – now. As children, they need the space and guidance to learn how to be self-cautioning, resilient, and self-sufficient people who love to learn, love to be challenged, love to learn from failure, and love to respect themselves and respect others. Your children, not you, will create their future.

Too often the popular message is that parents need to develop children into a self-functioning, fully sufficient 'adults' by providing them with a healthy sprinkle of love, care, and resources. But that misses the point of being a child. Children should be self-functioning, fully sufficient, and loved and cared for while they are still children. They should be encouraged and allowed to enjoy being a child. What better preparation could there be for a great and self-fulfilling adulthood than to enjoy the freedom, simplicity, and naivety of childhood.

The role of school

The focus of this book is on learning – how the child learns, how the parents learn, and how to enhance a love of learning in families. We talk about schools and your role as a parent in choosing schools and how to nurture learning during these years.

Long before school starts, parents are their child's first 'learners' (note the use of *learner*, not *teacher*). Being a parent and your child's 'first learner' is mostly about developing *your* ability to listen, set fair boundaries, and develop particular skills about how children learn. Next comes childcare and early pre-school settings, and then school starts – usually with much excitement for the child but followed by years of declining interest for most until they are 16. Lee Jenkins noted 95% of 4–6-year-olds want to go to school to learn, but by the end of elementary this drops to four out of ten, at best.[1]

Whether at school, at home, in the neighborhood, or among friends, parents want their children to have the skills to socialize and to understand the norms and cultures of the societies they live in. It is also desirable for children to understand how to be critical and to express that criticism of this very society, so they can improve it when they take over the reins. It's important, too, for children to respect themselves and respect others. And even more important is teaching them how to learn – the major theme of this book.

What this book is and what it is not

This book outlines the many ways of thinking that aim to help in the 'teaching' role parents play during early childhood, elementary, and high school days. A parent's job does not stop when children start school or when you drop them off at the school gate. While this book is about all the great things parents can do to support the learning life of their children, we do offer a warning: If you are reading this book to find out how to make your child the next prodigy, or believe that your child is gifted, multitalented, or any other label, or you want a perfect child – then sorry. Go read a fairy story.

Yes, you should believe that your child can do marvelous things. But the predictability of what a child can do as a child and what they can then do when they are an adult is not as high as many think – the very experience of growing up can get in the way of early predictions. Indeed, only about 5–10% of child prodigies become gifted adults, and most 'gifted' children do not become gifted adults. This is not because the childcare center or the school does not treat them as special enough but because they grow and change in their learning. The pressure of your expectations may not be shared or met by your child, particularly as the child's views and expectations become more and more important. Too often those labeled gifted in some areas find it difficult as teenagers to face failure and challenges in new domains of knowing, particularly with over-pressuring parents. If children do not learn how to cope with challenges, failures, and errors during infancy and childhood then they are poorly set up for later schooling and life. The aim is to let them enjoy the desirable struggles of learning while they are young, and let them strive for more challenging heights: Do not over inflate their gifts.

As you will see throughout this book, creating opportunities, providing challenges, and coping strategies are the best legacy you can give your child – they are lessons that they will take with them into adulthood.

The research evidence

A word about the research from which the messages in this book are derived. The evidence is drawn from John's extensive research program of the past 25-plus years on the influences which have the greatest positive effect on students' school-related learning. The research, known as the Visible Learning program, involved a synthesis of more than 1,600 meta-analyses composed of 100,000-plus studies, and involving 300 million students.[2] While the emphasis was on school-related student learning, the messages on the importance to student learning of teachers' mind frames apply equally to parents' mind frames toward learning. As preparation for this book on parenting, we also synthesized many studies on the influence of parenting. More information on the evidence base used for this book is provided in the Appendix for Visible Learning on achievement and the Appendix at the end of this book for the synthesis on parenting.

We also provide a glossary of terms at the end of the book.

The main messages – the 10 mind frames

Dr Benjamin Spock wrote the all-time best seller *Baby and Child Care*, which encouraged parents to see their children as individuals rather than the role of parenting being the rule keepers or having to follow a one-size-fits-all approach to parenting. Spock promoted the idea that parents should 'trust their instincts' and began his book with 'You know more than you think you do'.[3] His central message was 'while you are trusting yourself as a parent, remember also to trust your child'. This advice is as relevant today for your children's learning as it was when Spock first promoted it. What we know as parents is very much influenced by our culture, and a lot of what is 'common sense' of child-rearing can differ a lot across cultures.

Different societies and cultures have different notions of what it means to be a good person, what it means to raise children, and what it means to be successful. A quick review of parenting across cultures would show there is no right way – a lot depends on what you want your child to do when a child, when they become when a teenager, and when they are a young adult.

We want to make this clear: Childhood is 'the now' for the child, and life at these ages is not always preparation for a later stage, including as an adult. Your child will create their future, not you. They will reinvent the world, critique, and refine what you now know and the world they (and you) live in. You cannot predict their future, and you will not know the range and nature of many jobs and careers 20 years hence. This is why it is so important that you experience the joy and pains of seeing your child as a real person from the moment they are born. More than any other time in their lives, children live in the 'now'. Their childhood should be adventurous, a time to learn many learning and coping strategies, enjoy the 'dignity of risks', and flourish in a socially enriching experience. By 'dignity of risk' we mean allowing children the dignity of taking such risks as are needed to develop autonomy.

The outcomes of parenting relate to a child developing a sense of competence, respect for self and others, and having a degree of autonomy to act and be responsible for those actions. Such self-determination is a major outcome in Western society and much of what is written in this book aims for children to develop these attributes in the 'now', during their childhood, in preparation for when they will need to be even more autonomous in determining their actions, reactions, and futures.

However, there is one finding we cannot ignore. Imagine you have two children in your family – why is it they can they are so different, even though they are in the same family environment, with similar genetics, the same parents, and the same expectations? Each child brings a lot to the family equation. They can differ in personality, their reactions to situations, how they cope with problems, and their abilities. The child does not enter the family neutral, and we will investigate some of these attributes that lead to important differences among your children.

We also investigate the evidence on child rearing. First, here's what we found about the influences that impact learning and achievement. In our Visible Learning research synthesis, we analyzed more than 100,000 studies based on more than one-third of a billion students. The most fascinating finding is that almost everything done to improve a child's learning will improve their learning. However, this does not mean you should close this book and do whatever you want. Far from it. The message is the opposite: Be wary of people saying, 'This worked for me', or 'Here's what works', because this will only be right if all you want is to merely improve learning. For us, to merely 'improve learning' is setting the bar too low, and that is simply not good enough.

Instead of setting the bar low for school-related learning and asking 'What works to increase learning?' our claim is that we should be raising the bar and asking, 'What works *best* to increase learning?' It is the same with parenting-related learning; this book is based not just on 'any' positive effect but on effects that are higher-than-average positive effects. We want more than an average or below-average effect. We want to set the bar higher than just 'what works' and ask instead, 'What works best?'

We also discovered that those above-average effects in school-related learning had little to do with the structural influences (class size; ability grouping; type of school, such as charter, private, or public; nature of curriculum; presence and type of tests). Rather, it has nearly everything to do with 'how teachers think'. It is more the moment-by-moment judgments that teachers make about what to do next, when they consider what the child can already do or not do, that matters. We call this 'evaluative thinking'. Similarly, evaluative thinking is what matters most for parenting-related learning. It is the ways parents think that are important: We present these ways of thinking as 10 parenting mind frames for learning – ten critical ways in which parents need to think about their role, and which guide their actions and behaviors and how they talk and listen.

Our Visible Learning mantra for school-related learning is that learning becomes visible 'when teachers see learning through the eyes of students, and when students become their own teachers'. Similarly with parenting, it is when parents see the effects of their words, actions, encouragement, and expectations through the eyes of their children. If you want to be a better parent, learn to see what you look like, feel like, and do by imagining you are the child. Stand in their shoes and see their world to better understand how to parent. You do not have to agree with them, but you need to hear, feel, and show you understand their viewpoint. Your aim is to help the child become the parent so that when they have to make decisions (especially when you are not present), they can see their actions as others would, know how their actions affect others around them, and know what best to do next.

Each of the remaining chapters discusses the 10 mind frames, or ways of thinking, that are needed for a parent to develop a great learner. We believe it is not primarily what you do or which model of parenting you adopt but how you think about what you do as a parent. Children are adept at working out what you are thinking (sometimes regardless of what you say), and we are more consistent in how we think than in what we do.

The 10 mind frames follow:

1 **I have appropriately high expectations**
2 **I make reasonable demands and am highly responsive to my child**
3 **I am not alone**
4 **I develop my child's skill, will, and sense of thrill**
5 **I love learning**

6 **I know the power of feedback and that success thrives on errors**

7 **I am a parent, not a teacher**

8 **I expose my child to language, language, language**

9 **I appreciate that my child is not perfect, nor am I**

10 **I am an evaluator of my impact**

Next we introduce each mind frame before discussing them individually in more detail in the following chapters.

1 I have appropriately high expectations

Children are born into a world of expectations which form the basis of how they will interact, learn, and develop. Your expectations for your child matter. Supporting your child to become a great learner means setting expectations that are high but appropriately so – as the Goldilocks principle would have it:, not too hard, not too easy. We would also add, not too boring. To meet expectations a child needs to have developed an emotional bond with the parents – preferably one based on trust. This is known as attachment. This sense of attachment and trust allows the child to make mistakes, learn from them, and develop resilience and other attributes. A child also needs encouragement, a sense of fairness in how you react to them and your direction to learn right from wrong. Your role is not to make your child depend on you but to help them develop autonomy and a sense of competence

2 I make reasonable demands and am highly responsive to my child

The research over the past 40 years has made an important distinction between three methods of parenting – permissive, authoritarian, and authoritative.[4] A parent is rarely only one of the three, but many parents do have a dominant set of strategies they apply – and, more importantly, the child is aware of which set the parent applies. Permissive parenting gives much leeway to the child, allows them free rein, and ignores a lot of misbehavior. Authoritarian, or bossy, parenting engages in 'I am right, you are the child', sees the child as not able to make good decisions, and engages in verbal hostility and sometimes corporal punishment. Authoritative, or reasoning, parenting creates warmth and involvement, engages in appropriate reasoning and listening to the child, and creates a climate of trust and fairness. We are sure you can guess which method wins the race!

There are two issues to consider here: one minor, the other more serious. First, it is easy to confuse the terms *authoritarian* and *authoritative* because they sound so alike. For this reason, we prefer the term *reasoning parenting* to *authoritative*. The second and more serious issue is that the evidence for the reasoning parent being the most desirable is not as big an effect as would be expected. However, when you add being a 'listening parent' to that of being a 'reasoning parent', the effects go up considerably.

The desired reasoning and listening strategies relate to developing the child's autonomy and the skills of relating to others, and promoting competence. This is called 'self-determination' theory and has been well and widely researched as a desirable set of attributes in our Western world. A key to this development of self-determination is for parents to know the right time to deliver the right amount of the right messages to build the child's confidence and skills to be a learner. It is never one size fits all. And the best answer is always considering what the right message, amount, and timing are from the world view of the child. Put yourselves in your child's shoes, learn to walk around in these shoes, and then imagine what the child is thinking, whether they have the skills and confidence, and what they would likely do. Then go back into your parent shoes and modify the message – recall you are meant to be a better thinker than your child, so think, react, and repurpose your message and give them food for thought.

3 I am not alone

You are not alone. The world today is one of instant connections to billions, where oceans and borders are no longer barriers, and often with a tyranny of closeness. Parents have oodles of websites, forums, Facebook advice, and so much more to advise them – not that this is necessarily a good thing given the often inconsistent and conflicting advice, which may or may not be based on valid and reliable evidence. It's easy to find something that will reinforce existing beliefs.

Further, your child is not alone. Children are brought up in a huge village today, with siblings, friends, avatars, television, and sometimes imaginary friends. It is through others that your child's world view can expand dramatically, make them so different from each other, and from whom they learn so much. Indeed, making friends is among the most important learning for a child – a lonely child is a horrible scenario. The skills of friendship can be taught particularly by parents modeling friendships with other adults.

When children are about to become adolescents, the importance of friends increases exponentially. This is because the purpose of friendship changes – a friend now becomes a soul mate, a person to share stories and confidences with, a person to try out ideas and who can give and withstand rebuffs and who can enhance your child's sense of self. We call this phase 'reputation enhancement'. Building a reputation is important to teenagers – it is how they want their peers to see them. For those adolescents who have built a reputation to be enhanced by peers, this has its ups and downs. More worrying, though, are those adolescents who do not have a reputation to enhance: This more than likely means they won't have friends, and life can be a lonely place for them.

4 I develop my child's skill, will, and sense of thrill

Children develop three major dimensions of learning that they bring to each encounter with you, and to their learning opportunities. The first is their skills, such as prior achievement, intellectual capabilities, working memory, culture and ethnic background and values, and 'executive functioning' (how we think and process information). The second is their will, or disposition, such as confidence to take on challenges, resilience, resourcefulness, reflectiveness, and relating.[5] The third is their sense of thrill, or their motivation to engage, persist, and complete learning tasks. Parents' role is to develop each of these dimensions of learning, and it is a bonus if there is overlap across them. Thus, high achievement at school may not be sufficient, or may even be negative, if the child does not also have the thrill to master and dive deeply into learning or the resilience to cope with failure and unknown situations and problems. Similarly, having a high passion for a topic without enhancing the skill and a willingness to take on new challenges can lead to disappointment. Parents need to develop all three attributes in children – the skill, the will, and the thrill.

5 I love learning

Children do not come into this world with fully formed brains. It is not correct to claim that babies are born with certain amounts of intelligence and talents and that the parents' role is to help realize those talents. This is because the brain undergoes major changes after birth – indeed even while you are reading these words. We begin to describe these changes by reviewing a more than 50-year-old argument put by the Swiss psychologist Jean Piaget. He once was influential in describing how the child changed so much over the years, and his findings still have credibility today.

Jean Piaget undertook some fascinating studies.[6] For example, he showed children how to pour a beaker of water into a wide but not tall glass and then into a narrow tall glass. The amount of water did not change, but children up to about 4–5 years of age would swear black and blue that the tall glass had more water. Only after their brains developed to a certain point could they appreciate that it was the same amount of water. He conducted many studies showing how children reasoned differently and proposed four major stages that children grow through. Of course, he had his critics, and today his work is mostly taught in child development as being of historical interest. For our purposes, however, we introduce some of Jean Piaget's findings to help you see as a parent the different world views that your child can have.

We go further and outline our own recent work tracing the way the brain changes in terms of 'executive functioning' – fancy words, yes, but a powerful concept. Executive functioning is mainly related to how we think and process information, and there are three major components.[7]

The first component is the ability to resist impulsive actions and avoid being distracted (known as 'inhibition'). This skill of being able to concentrate without being distracted, and of being able to inhibit impulsive behavior, is a learned skill and does not occur in meaningful ways until a child is about 7 years plus. The second component is 'shifting' (also known as 'cognitive flexibility' or 'task shifting') is the ability to switch between tasks, while the third is 'monitoring and updating', or building the skills to organize and manipulate the contents in your working memory. If you were given a list of items to buy when you went to the grocery store and you did not write the items down, most people would recall about four to six items from such a list – people have limited working memory. These three components of executive functioning are covered in more detail in a later chapter.

To return to Jean Piaget – modern neuroscience has provided some of the reasons children go through his four stages, which relate to their developing skills in the three components of executive functioning. We think it powerful for parents to stop and listen to how their child is reasoning and how they are explaining their actions. Parents can then create demands and structure tasks suited to a child's level and capabilities in executive functioning.

Jean Piaget[8] wrote much about the importance of play to a child's development, maintaining it builds a child's communication, social, and cognitive skills as well as helping them learn to take the role of others and to recall past experience for present use. Games with rules require higher levels of social skills. This, and similar claims, have led many to claim play is critical to learning. But is it? Play can be a worthwhile activity in itself but play for learning requires much skill to set up and enact. We will look later at the research on play to build a balanced argument about the place of play for learning, but for now we note – play is fun, and having fun is critical to childhood.

Computer games are one form of play that many parents had limited involvement with in their childhood days. While there is much debate about when children should be exposed to screens (much like the warning in earlier times against children watching too much television), the developers of computer games certainly have been fast learners about how to make learning fun. It is worth considering how they do this, as it can show how to make parenting more fun.

Another child development guru who has had a lasting legacy is Lev Vygotsky.[9] He placed much value on the social environment and social interactions and how children learn values about culture and learning through dialogue. One of his more powerful notions was the 'zone of proximal development' – this zone includes all the ideas, activities, and skills a child is ready to learn *next* – not by themselves but with the help of a more advanced 'teacher' or parent. There is little place for the notion that children should be left to discover for themselves or to be in control of their learning as this leads to stagnation, with little growth and little confidence in facing new challenges. When children are left on their own, they are not necessarily aware of the next best challenges and tend to redo what they can do already, thus indulging in doing more of the same thing rather than doing something better or differently. It is important to always look for the learning zone ahead of your child.

6   I know the power of feedback and that success thrives on errors

Many years ago, I (John) published an article with the phrase 'All you need to maximize learning is dollops of feedback'. The New Zealand government picked up on this, creating posters using this phrase that were sent to all schools. I now regret making this comment, as it is not the right message. It is not giving 'dollops' of feedback that is important. Children already receive dollops of feedback. What is important is not the feedback given but how that feedback is received.

Feedback is a powerful tool – if it is used appropriately. The important point about feedback is not what feedback is given but how that feedback is received. Take schools as one example: Teachers may give kids a lot of feedback, but most kids only receive a few seconds of feedback a day. So, the issue is, How can you increase the reception of the feedback? You will already know from experience that many a time you have told your child to do this or not do that – and they are not listening. Children, like adults, are good at selective listening. In the chapter on this mind frame, we talk about the costs of receiving feedback, the best ways to ensure that feedback is received, and the most powerful kinds of feedback. We also show you how you can listen better to feedback from your child and how this skill has more effect on your child than most other skills.

A major review by Avraham Kluger and Angelo DeNisi showed that about one-third of feedback has either no effect or a negative effect.[10] It also shows that the feedback you give to your child may work one day but the same feedback may not work the next and that the same feedback you give one child may work for them but does not work for another child. Understanding this variability is critical for getting the most from the power of feedback. A key is to focus on how your feedback is being heard, understood, and actioned. Your child builds skills to interpret feedback, to ignore it, to develop selective listening, and to know how to use it to improve. Sometimes, your child can hear and understand the feedback but not know how to activate it, and they may need further feedback on how to improve. Also, including praise in feedback can dilute the effectiveness of the feedback – try giving a feedback 'sandwich' (two dollops of praise and a corrective), wait a day so your child is not merely using short-term memory, and then ask your child what they recall about the feedback you gave them yesterday – they will recall the praise and struggle with the feedback information.

7 I am a parent, not a teacher

We make a major distinction between the role of parents and that of teachers. Teachers are at school and parents are at home. You are not the school teacher. Your job is to support your children in their learning in school but not to do the teacher's job. There are major ways you can provide this support – most of all by promoting the language of learning – that is, helping your child see what is involved in being a successful learner. Supporting your children in their learning at school involves helping your children see struggle as a positive term and failures as a learner's best friend. It involves promoting feedback, both to and from your children, as a desirable skill, and encouraging the joys of discovery and curiosity.

Probably one of the most discussed questions (particularly when meeting other parents) is how to choose a pre-school or school. It is a big decision if for no other reason than, once chosen, it is tough to change. There is a dilemma in that choosing a school is a parental decision, but choosing the teacher is a school decision – and it is the teacher who really matters.

Your key role as a parent is NOT to re-create school at home but to adopt Goldilocks's notions of expectations – not too high, not too low – for your child's learning. Then parents can take major roles in demonstrating what it means to be successful in the learning, that is, showing the child what success looks like before they immerse themselves in the learning. For example, instead of 'clean your room', say 'in cleaning your room there should be nothing left on the floor, everything is put away in drawers, and your bed is tidy'. These 'success criteria' not only help make the nature of the task clear, but they also provide a benchmark for when 'good is good enough'. It also provides a goal for you and them to evaluate their success. Consider not giving a sense of what success looks like: Would you go outside and jump the high jump knowing that there was NO bar across to show you what success looks like? Would you play Angry Birds or Pokémon Go if you did not know what success was in these games? Would you watch tennis or football if there was not such concept as 'points' or 'goals' or what it means to be successful?

8 I expose my child to language, language, language

Learning is very much a function of language. Talking, listening, and speaking are core features in classrooms and need to be a core feature in the home also. From the very beginning children need to be exposed to language, language, language – that is, exposed to talking, listening, reasoning, explaining.

Here's a question. Imagine two children. One, Adam, is born into a family where the child is *not* exposed to much talking, listening, reasoning, explaining. Another, Aaron, is born into a family where there is a lot of talking, listening, reasoning, explaining. Now imagine these two children at age 5 and starting school. How many words will Aaron have heard MORE than Adam? That is, how many more words will Aaron have been exposed to by the time he starts school compared to Adam? Answer: Thirty million.[11] Wow. No wonder Aaron has a head start, no wonder we emphasize how critical it is to surround children with language. But note, it is the *interaction* of this talking that matters – not passively watching television or playing games but interacting.

The *Matthew effect* is a term coined from a verse in the New Testament (Matthew 25:29), which is commonly paraphrased as 'the rich get richer and the poor get poorer'; that is, further opportunities come to those who are already advantaged while for those who are already disadvantaged, that disadvantage compounds. This effect applies to our children too. If by the age of 8 your child does not have a level of literacy and numeracy considered 'minimal', it will become hard for them to ever catch up. This is why we place such emphasis on the power of language and on parents' role in promoting language in the home (particularly in the first five years). Your role is to create, find, and welcome situations where there are high levels of interaction using language. This is the reason all parents should read books to their children as this expands the range of language they hear. Talking, listening, reasoning, explaining – these are the building blocks of learning.

9 I appreciate that my child is not perfect, nor am I

The roles of parents and their children have changed greatly over the past 50 years or so. Parents have become more protective; rarely are children allowed to roam the street on the condition they are home for dinner, children are driven everywhere, and walking to school is frowned on. There are many helicopter, snowplow, jet-fighter, snowflake, magic bullet, and bonsai parents.

There is no perfection in parenting, and no child is perfect – the world has not only dangers but also opportunities, has not only risks and weird people but also wonderful potential friends and allies. Parents need to guard against overly protective parenting. Children need skills to evaluate situations and people and to evaluate and mitigate risk. This requires parenting that teaches children the 'dignity of risks' and the skills of when and how to say no.

10 I am an evaluator of my impact

When we speak with teachers about professional development, we tell them, 'We do not care how you teach, we care about the impact of your teaching'. The same argument applies to parenting – it is the impact on your children that matters, not the purity of any parenting method. By impact we mean parents having a positive effect on their children's learning, such that their children have multiple learning strategies, know their current levels of understanding, and are clear about where they are going toward successful learning. It means developing children who are confident to take on challenges and can select tools to guide their learning. And it means children who seek, understand, and use feedback; recognize errors are opportunities to learn; can monitor their progress and adjust their learning; and can interact with others in their learning. To develop these attributes, the home needs to be open to learning, engage in collective problem-solving, welcome failure as the learner's best friend, and ensure that the Goldilocks principle of challenges and expectations is understood and enacted – that is, parents must set challenges and expectations that are not too hard, not too easy, and not too boring. All this may seem forbidding, but recall Dr Spock's advice – parents know more than they think they do, and there is no one right way.

Concluding comments

This book is about parenting to create great learners. There is a strong focus on learning: what it means, how to know it is happening, and what the core skills of learning are. We do not talk much about the content of the learning especially at the school level – whether it should include other languages, or music, or certain aspects of math, and so on. It's not that these are unimportant, but rather they are not the focus of this book. Our message is simple: Learn to listen, learn to surround your child with language and thinking aloud from an early age, understand how your child thinks, and enjoy the wonder as they change their thinking as they grow. If you wish your child to learn these perspectives, you need also to see the world through their eyes, their ways of thinking, and their ways of learning. Successful parenting involves adults seeing themselves through the eyes of their children, and children learning to become their own teachers.

Notes

1 Jenkins, L. (2015). *Optimize your school: It's all about the strategy*. Corwin Press.

2 **Visible Learning overviews:**

Hattie, J. A. C. (2009). *Visible learning: A synthesis of 800+ meta-analyses on achievement*. Routledge.

Hattie, J. A. C. (2012). *Visible learning for teachers: Maximizing impact on achievement*. Routledge.

Hattie, J. A. C., & Anderman, E. (2013). *Handbook on student achievement*. Routledge.

Hattie, J. A. C., & Yates, G. (2014). *Visible learning and the science of how we learn*. Routledge.

Hattie, J. A. C., Masters, D., & Birch, K. (2016). *Visible learning into action*. Routledge.

Hattie, J. A. C., & Zierer, K. (2018). *10 mindframes for visible learning*. Routledge.

Hattie, J., & Smith, R. (Eds.). (2020). *10 mindframes for leaders: The visible learning approach to school success*. Corwin Press.

Hattie, J. A. C., & Anderman, E. (2020). *Visible learning: Guide to student achievement – schools edition*. Routledge.

Rickards, F., Hattie, J. A. C., & Reid, C. (2021). *The turning point: Growing expertise, evaluative thinking, and the future of the teaching profession*. Routledge.

Hattie, J. A. C., & Larsen, S. (2020). *The purposes of education: In conversation*. Routledge.

Hattie, J. A. C., & Zierer, Z. (2020). *Visible learning insights*. Routledge.

Hattie, J. A. C., Bustamante, V., Almarode, J., Fisher, D., & Frey, N. (2021). *Great teaching by design: From intention to implementation in the Visible Learning Classroom*. Corwin Press.

Specific aspects of Visible Learning

Hattie, J. A. C., & Clarke, S. (2019). *Visible learning: Feedback*. Routledge.

Frey, N., Hattie, J. A. C., & Fisher, D. (2018). *Developing assessment capable learners*. Corwin Press.

Hattie, J. A. C., Clarke, S., Fisher, D., & Frey, N. (2021). *Collective student efficacy*. Corwin Press.

Applied to curricula domains

Fisher, D., Frey, N., & Hattie, J. A. C. (2016). *Visible learning for literacy, grades K–12: Implementing the practices that work best to accelerate student learning.* Corwin Press.

Hattie, J. A. C., Fisher, D., Frey, N., Gojak, L. M., Moore, S. D., & Mellman, W. (2017). *Visible learning for mathematics, grades K–12: What works best to optimize student learning.* Corwin Press.

Almarode, J. T., Fisher, D., Frey, N., & Hattie, J. A. C. (2018). *Visible learning in science, grades K–12: What works best to optimize student learning.* Corwin Press.

Fisher, D., Frey, N., Hattie, J., & Amador-Valerio, O. (2019). *Visible learning for English language learners.* Corwin Press.

Hattie, J. A. C., Stern, J., Fisher, D., & Frey, N. (2020). *Visible learning for social studies, grades K–12: Designing student learning for conceptual understanding.* Corwin Press.

Applied to distance learning

Fisher, D., Frey, N., Bustamante, V. J., & Hattie, J. (2021). *Assessment playbook for distance blended learning.* Corwin Press.

Fisher, D., Frey, N., Almarode, J. T., & Hattie, J. A. C. (2021). *The distance learning playbook for college and university instruction.* Corwin Press.

Fisher, D., Frey, N., & Hattie, J. (2021). *The distance learning playbook grades K–12: Instruction: Teaching for engagement and impact in any setting.* Corwin Press.

Fisher, D., Frey, N., Almarode, J., Hattie, J., & Wiseman, R. (2021). *The distance learning playbook parents: Teaching for engagement and impact in any setting.* Corwin Press.

Fisher, D., Frey, N., Smith, D., & Hattie, J. A. C. (2021). *Rebound. Grades K-12: A playbook for rebuilding agency, accelerating learning recovery, and rethinking schools.* Corwin Press.

Fisher, D., Frey, N., Smith, D., & Hattie, J. A. C. (2021). *Leading the Rebound: 20+ must-dos to restart teaching and learning.* Corwin Press.

3 Spock, B. (1946). *The common sense book of baby and child care.* Duell, Sloan & Pearce.

4 Baumrind, D. (1968). Authoritarian vs. authoritative parental control. *Adolescence, 3*(11), 255.

5 Claxton, G. (2017). *The learning power approach: Teaching learners to teach themselves.* Corwin Press.

6 Piaget, J. (1964). Cognitive development in children: Piaget. *Journal of Research in Science Teaching, 2*(3), 176–186; Piaget, J. (2013). *The construction of reality in the child* (Vol. 82). Routledge.

7 Miyake, A., & Friedman, N. P. (2012). The nature and organisation of individual differences in executive functions: Four general conclusions. *Current Directions in Psychological Science*, *21*, 8–14. doi:10.1177/0963721411429458

8 Piaget, J. (1962). *Play, dreams and imitation in childhood*. The Norton Library.

9 Moll, L. C. (2013). *LS Vygotsky and education*. Routledge.

10 Kluger, A. N., & DeNisi, A. (1996). The effects of feedback interventions on performance: A historical review, a meta-analysis, and a preliminary feedback intervention theory. *Psychological Bulletin*, *119*(2), 254.

11 Hart, B., & Risley, T. R. (2003). The early catastrophe: The 30 million word gap by age 3. *American Educator*, *27*(1), 4–9. And see Sperry, D. E., Sperry, L. L., & Miller, P. J. (2019). Reexamining the verbal environments of children from different socioeconomic backgrounds. *Child Development*, *90*(4), 1303–1318.

PART

Setting the scene

I have appropriately high expectations

1 *Children are born into a world of expectations*

- These expectations form the basis of how your child will interact, learn, and develop.

- To be successful in meeting these expectations they will need encouragement and demand a sense of fairness in how you react to them.

2 *The Goldilocks principle of expectations and encouragement*

- The aim is to make these expectations appropriately challenging, socially appropriate, and adhering to the Goldilocks principle of not too easy, not too hard, and not too boring.

- If you set expectations too low, they probably will achieve them – and that's it; set them too high and they may try for a time to meet them but ultimately will throw them away through fatigue and helplessness at trying to reach what is not attainable.

3 *Attachment builds expectations*

- Attachment relates to a child's emotional connection to an adult caregiver – when needing comfort, support, nurturance, protection, or learning, particularly in times of distress and confusion.

- To meet expectations, children require high levels of trust so that they can explore, make mistakes, learn from errors; develop resilience; and know when to seek help, when to be conscientious, when to stop and learn from others, and when and how to seek, hear, and deal with feedback.

- Your role is not to make your child depend on you or to follow all your instructions but to develop their sense and skills in *autonomy* and their sense of *competence*.

DOI: 10.4324/9781003257028-2

This chapter outlines the importance of having high expectations for your child, ensuring that these are challenging, and creating a family environment of high trust so that your child can explore, make mistakes, and develop resilience.

My (KH) firstborn, Emma, at 4 years old was an exceptional child (I know all parents think this, as they should). She was climbing ladders before she could walk, she was talking in full sentences before her first birthday, and her curious and inquisitive nature leaves her wanting to know more about the world around her. With my youngest, Danielle, I was constantly comparing her timeline to Emma's. I know that my children are different, and I celebrate their unique qualities and behaviors every day. I want them each to be their own person and yet I still compare. Emma was walking at 10 months; Danielle still preferred to crawl. Emma was talking in full sentences before her first birthday Danielle, at 16 months, was still not stringing sentences together. Emma loves creating and Danielle loves creating a mess. I have high expectations for both my girls and want them to do well and learn as much as they can, but I have forgotten the key word in that sentence. 'I have high expectations' — the word I am missing is appropriate. The expectations I had for Danielle are not fair. Of course she is not progressing at the same rate as Emma, and that is okay. She is not progressing the same because she is not Emma. Danielle may not be talking yet, but what are my expectations for Danielle? She is curious and loves exploring her surroundings. Danielle is amazingly resilient. She will be running as she is playing and fall, but that doesn't faze her. She just gets up and continues to keep going. As a parent I need to be thinking about what my expectations are for each of my children and are they acceptable for them.

The power of expectations can dominate how your child grows up in the many worlds they face. Even if you do not say these expectations aloud, your children soon become deeply aware of your expectations for them. They become aware of expectations from the earliest ages as they form boundaries, during elementary schools when they learn to comply, in adolescence when they stretch and question, and in early adulthood as they take over deciding, building, and realizing the expectations they have learned from you, tested you with, and developed for themselves. The aim is to make these expectations appropriately challenging and socially appropriate and adhere to the Goldilocks principle of not too easy, not too hard, and not too boring.

One of the more famous experiments in education was conducted by Robert Rosenthal and Lenore Jacobsen[1] and was termed 'the Pygmalion effect'. Pygmalion was a Greek sculptor who fell in love with a statue of a beautiful woman he had carved. He kissed and doted on the statue, which then turned into a woman, and his expectations were realized. Similarly, in their experiment, Rosenthal and Jacobsen told teachers that half their students would 'bloom' during the year and half would not. All students were tested before the split and then divided into bloomers and non-bloomers. But the teachers did not know that the division into bloomers and non-bloomers was random and not based on the test results. Sure enough, at the end of the year, the bloomers outperformed the non-bloomers. Given the assignment of bloomer/non-bloomer was random, the researchers concluded the difference was because the teachers had higher expectations for these bloomers. Like most research that tells bold stories, this one too has been extensively criticized, but the basic message has often been replicated.[2]

This research led to many hunting for the sources of these expectations. The list of potential sources is a long one. It includes gender, ethnicity, social class, stereotypes, diagnostic labels, and physical attractiveness. It includes language style, the age of the student, personality, and social skills. And it includes the relationship between teacher and student background, names, other siblings, and one-parent background. Christine Rubie-Davies[3] argued that this hunt for specific influences was not that worthwhile, because teachers who have high expectations tend to have them for all the students, and those who have low expectations tend to have low expectations for all the students. She tested the students and gave the teachers the results, and encouraged the teachers to do their own evaluations in the first month of the school year. She then asked the teachers to predict the students' attainment at the end of the year. She found that some teachers had high expectations of yearly progress for all students in the class whereas others had low expectations and that both groups realized their teachers' expectations – wonderfully (for the highs) and sadly (for the lows).

This chapter outlines how to encourage appropriately high expectations, how to provide encouragement for the child to realize these expectations, and how to develop the child's coping strategies to deal with your expectations.

1 Children are born into a world of expectations

Children enter a world of expectations – from parents, from grandparents, from almost anyone who comes into contact with the child. These expectations are the basis of how your child will interact, learn, and develop. Without expectations, the child is in a more random world, not knowing when good is good enough and not appreciating the possibilities for progress instead of doing what is minimal. Higher expectations can offer opportunities, entice more effort and striving, and help children realize the thrill of playing the game and meeting the challenge.

Their perception of your expectations starts early. Between 1–3 years, they are rapidly developing a 'theory of mind', or way of seeing the world around them, learning how to interact and to act in light of others, how to make sense of this world, how to develop competence, and how to learn to make choices. This all requires high levels of trust because children are vulnerable in these early years, hence the importance of having a sense of attachment, or emotional connection, so they can build this trust to explore, make mistakes, and learn from errors. They are learning the importance of how to cope with situations – both emotional coping (crying, venting) and problem-based coping (restructuring what happened, knowing how to learn effectively). To do this they need to have a sense of persistence and know when to have grit and when to seek help, when to be conscientious and when to stop and learn from others, and when and how to seek, hear, and deal with feedback.

During the early years, parents need 'to be in front', but as children grow, parents need to gradually release responsibility, moving to be beside the child. The early communication of appropriately high expectations sets the building blocks for the all-to-critical adolescent years – when they spend much more time away from you.

Most of us have expectations or heard stories about what it is like to parent teenagers! The concept of 'adolescence' has been around for many centuries and means to grow into maturity. Stanley Hall wrote the definitive book *Adolescence* in 1904,[4] and he was intrigued by the German notion of 'sturm and drang' or storm and stress. He portrayed adolescence as going through a negative phase, fluctuating emotions, selfishness, and altruism, good and bad conduct, insensitivity and apathy, mood disruptions, risky behaviors, and parental conflict. It has taken a long time to correct these messages, as adolescence does not have to be a period of storm and stress, particularly if the adolescent has learned boundaries, that home is still a safe haven, and the appropriateness of expectations. Here's the tough news. Teenage years now cover a longer age period and many new labels are being invented: tweenagers (9–12), teenagers (13–19), and twentagers (20–27), with adolescence stopping more at 27 than 19.

2 The Goldilocks principle of expectations and encouragement

Goldilocks was right. Expectations must not be too high, too low, or too boring. We used to say, 'Not too high, and not too low', but then realized that many will strive for higher goals if the tasks are not boring. Also, you may need to work with your children to revise your expectations – and appreciate that they TOO have a major say in setting these expectations. But be warned, if you set them too low, they probably will achieve them – and that's it; too high and they may meet them for a while but then throw them away through fatigue at trying (a typical reaction to Tiger Mom parenting).

It is even better if there is some agreement between parents and children in the content and focus of the high expectations and in the joint nurturing and encouragement between mothers and fathers with their children. Any discrepancies can increase unease and discord and will certainly be picked up by the child. It may be that some parents (especially fathers) may see their role as 'father-as-helper', but today more fathers now want to be highly involved in the care and growth of their children as providers and teachers. They want, like many adults in the lives of children, to be helpful, close, and have emotional bonds – and not only hold appropriately high expectations but also help their children realize these expectations.

Twenty years ago, fathers were available for one-quarter as often as mothers in two-parent families, and their main role was the provision of resources. The dad's involvement increases if the father's friends are also involved with their children and when the workplace supports active involvement. A major message throughout this book is the beauties and wonder of fathering – the two of us thoroughly enjoy it, gain more than we give, and have the option of prioritizing time for fathering that may be denied to some.

Children are adept at coping with different expectations from different sources (moms, dads, teachers, peers, etc.). As they grow, they become more adept at seeking different sources of support, begin to look to peers more, and create different worlds within the family, at school, and on the playground.

I (JH) always recall Heather, a wonderful girl in my Year 6 class – quiet, helpful, diligent, and on task. Then I met her mother, whose first words at the first parent–teacher meeting were 'Is she as big a b**** at school as she is at home'. School was Heather's haven, and she had learned to cope quite differently at school than at home and had quite different expectations of how she interacted, spoke, and behaved. The resourcefulness and adaptability she had developed (herself) during elementary years would help her much as she negotiated being a teenager in her home. I still recall Heather as one of the pleasures of being a teacher.

3 Attachment builds expectations

A precursor to realizing any expectations is a healthy bond between parents and child – preferably one based on trust. This notion of 'feeling attached' has dominated much of the research literature about children and families since the early work by John Bowlby, a British psychologist. He noted that 'the infant and young child should experience a warm, intimate, and continuous relationship with his mother (or permanent mother substitute) in which both find satisfaction and enjoyment' and that 'not to do so may have significant and irreversible mental health consequences'.[5] This does mean, as many critics claimed at the time, that the mother should always be in the home and not at work, that children should never be sent to day care, or that others than mothers could not provide such attachment. But it did focus attention on asking about attachment from the child's perspective – how did they feel 'attached'.

So, what is attachment? John Bowlby[6] claimed it was 'a strong disposition to seek proximity to and contact with a specific figure and to do so in certain situations, notably when frightened, tired or ill', that is, being close, comforting, and building trust. Attachment relates to a child's emotional connection to an adult caregiver – an attachment figure. It relates to their turning selectively to that adult to increase closeness when needing comfort, support, nurturance, or protection, and so is most evident in times of distress and confusion. What does your child do when stressed?

A newborn child can attach to many adults, but at about 2–6 months this begins to change as the child seeks some predictability from their environment: 'Who looks after me when I am stressed? Who best meets my needs when I cry out? Who do I turn to if some things happen that I do not like or understand?' If there is no such adult figure to turn to, this can lead to withdrawal, fear of being in new environments, a lack of risk-taking and exploration, and not learning from mistakes – all key skills that will pay back huge dividends later in children's learning lives.

It used to be claimed that a lack of attachment was to be related to being in foster homes or parents getting divorced. But it was soon realized that it was the quality and nature of attachment that mattered, and these changes did not necessarily mean attachment did not happen – in some cases there was less attachment before the child went into these new situations. Close contact, continuing routines (e.g., for sleeping, waking, feeding, and activities), using familiar toys, and reducing exposure to adult conflict all help develop attachment in times of change.

A recent meta-analysis by Sheri Madigan and colleagues[7] showed how John Bowlby's attachment notions are still relevant today. The likelihood of poor attachment as an infant increased the risk of later negative behaviors by about 300%. Attachment in these 0–2-year period can have enduring effects on later social relationships and on emotional and behavioral patterns of behavior. These early patterns can be repeated when the child encounters other adults, such as teachers, other caregivers, siblings. The argument is that the child internalizes how they deal with conflict, new situations, and new threats in their environment that can lead to positive and negative attributes that can be internalized (such as anxiety, helplessness, depression, conduct disorders, anger, and frustration) or externalized (aggression, naughty behavior). Who does your child turn to in moments of distress and uncomfortableness? It is likely that what they did in these circumstances between 0–2 sets up this reaction. The critical issue here is a child's perceptions and understanding of their own beliefs and feelings, more so than adult reports of these. The important thing is how the child reacts to new and uncomfortable situations and to stress, not how the parents perceive and deal with this reaction.

Concluding comments

The message is be aware of your expectations, ensure they are not set too high or too low and that they are transparent so your child does not have to 'guess' what you are expecting, and then your parenting role is to help and encourage your child met these expectations. These expectations can change over time, but always consider that your power is seeing opportunities for higher performance in the child they may not see in themselves. Certainly, if you set your expectations too low, many children can become frustrated, bored, and sadly live down to these lower expectations; and if too high may overperform to gain your attention and support but this may tax them over time and ultimately they will rebel. To realize appropriately challenging expectations requires an emotional connection between parent and child, and such attachment entails comfort, support, nurturance, protection, or learning, particularly in times of distress and confusion. This bonding leads to high levels of trust so that your child can explore, make mistakes, learn from errors; develop resilience; and know when to seek help, when to be conscientious, when to stop and learn from others, and when and how to seek, hear, and deal with feedback. And learn to do these learning tasks even when you are not present with them, hence developing their autonomy as great learners.

Notes

1 Rosenthal, R., & Jacobson, L. (1992). *Pygmalion in the classroom* (Expanded ed.). Irvington.
2 Good, T. L., Sterzinger, N., & Lavigne, A. (2018). Expectation effects: Pygmalion and the initial 20 years of research. *Educational Research and Evaluation, 24*(3–5), 99–123; Weinstein, R. S. (2018). Pygmalion at 50: Harnessing its power and application in schooling. *Educational Research and Evaluation, 24*(3–5), 346–365; Spitz, H. H. (1999). Beleaguered Pygmalion: A history of the controversy over claims that teacher expectancy raises intelligence. *Intelligence, 27*(3), 199–234.
3 Rubie-Davies, C. (2014). *Becoming a high expectation teacher: Raising the bar.* Routledge.
4 Hall, G. S. (1904). *Adolescence: Its psychology and its relations to physiology, anthropology, sociology, sex, crime, religion, and education* (Vols. 1 & 2). Appleton.
5 Bowlby, J. (1951). *Maternal care and mental health.* World Health Organization.
6 Bowlby, J. (1969). *Attachment and loss. Vol. 1: Attachment* (2nd ed., p. 371). Basic Books.
7 Madigan, S., Brumariu, L. E., Villani, V., Atkinson, L., & Lyons-Ruth, K. (2016). Representational and questionnaire measures of attachment: A meta-analysis of relations to child internalizing and externalizing problems. *Psychological Bulletin, 142*(4), 367.

2

I make reasonable demands and am highly responsive to my child

1 *I am a reasonable parent and a great listener*

- You need to be trusted, seen as reliable, be clear in what you say and mean, and show a high level of confidence and respect for your child. In the jargon, you need to be authoritative and teach your child to become authoritative. And do not confuse authoritative (being reasonable) with authoritarian (forcing obedience) or permissive (affirming, nonpunitive, laissez-faire).

- Reasonable parenting involves being *seen by your child* to be a great listener, reasonable, trusted, reliable, and dependable so that your child will also develop these attributes, and becomes a great learner.

2 *The importance of developing self-determination*

- Developing self-determination requires a gradual release of responsibility for learning from the parent to the child so they will develop autonomy, skills in relating, and competence.

3 *The need to develop coping strategies*

- A critical role of parents is to help the child build strategies to cope with unexpected, unsuccessful, or failed or thwarted expectations. Coping aims to prevent or reduce threat, harm, and loss and thus reduce distress.

- Coping relates to the child's sense of challenge, and their strategies will change over time.

DOI: 10.4324/9781003257028-3

■ There is a need to teach both *problem-focused coping* and *emotion-focused coping*. Problem-focused coping is directed at the stressor itself. It involves taking steps to remove or to evade the stressor, or to diminish its impact. Emotion-focused coping minimizes distress triggered by stressors.

This chapter introduces the idea of great parenting as being seen by your child as responsive and a good listener. You want the same responsiveness and listening from your child. The aim is to develop skills in autonomy (so they act and react the same outside as inside the home, when you are not present), relating to others (including respect for self and others), and enhance their competence to strive in their world.

1 I am a reasonable parent and a great listener

How to be a parent whom the child trusts – and respects – and (most often) obeys? How to be a parent with an authoritative air, commanding and self-confident? How to be responsive, a great listener, and a source of trust and guidance? These are the qualities of an authoritative parent or, to use a simpler term, a reasonable and listening parent. Reasonable is not exactly the same as authoritative but is easier to say, is less likely to be confused with authoritarian, and conveys our duty to build reason and develop the trust that leads to being seen as reasonable. It conveys our duty to be a great listener, and even when we do not explain our reasons (and sometimes we should not), being reasonable portrays a sense of rightness that we would want our children to also develop and emulate.

For the past 40 years, the research has found support for the authoritative/reasonable type of parenting as the most effective.[1] What does it mean, and how is it different from other types of parenting? And, critically, reasoning and listening about what, when, and how?

Let's start with the meaning of authoritative: 'Able to be trusted, reliable, dependable, likely to be respected'. So, reasonable. Note the interesting switch here – it is not the parent seeing the child as having these attributes but the child seeing the parent as having these attributes. This underlines an important message from our Visible Learning research in classrooms – learning is maximized when teachers see learning through the eyes of the students. Similarly, child development is maximized in families when parents see parenting through the eyes of their children.

This form of parenting is quite different from many other forms. In 1966 Diane Baumrind introduced an important distinction between permissive, authoritarian, and authoritative parents.[iv] To paraphrase her three forms of parenting:

Authoritarian parents aim to shape, control, and evaluate the child. They aim to mold the child to their set of standards and value obedience as a virtue and punishment or shame as a tool to achieve these standards. The standards can be high (as in the Tiger Mum) or low (you can be slovenly like me), but the child is to be seen and not heard, has low levels of autonomy, and needs to learn their place in the hierarchy of the home and society. Authoritarian parents are endowed with greater wisdom, know what is right, and the child should accept their place in this world. The parents are in the castle; the child is at the gate.

Permissive parents are free spirits: 'The child will emerge from their chrysalis of childhood in their own time and in their own way'. These parents behave in a nonpunitive, accepting, and affirming manner; consult with the child; and give plenty of explanations for family rules. The permissive parent encourages the child to see the parent as a resource to be used, not necessarily an ideal to emulate nor a source for shaping or altering the child's ongoing behavior or thoughts. The child is given high levels of autonomy, is expected to have increasing control over their learning, and is hardly ever subject to parental power to make decisions.

Authoritative parents are in between. They do provide direction for the child, encourage verbal give-and-take, share reasoning, and solicit objections but do not always give in without restrictions. These parents aim to develop autonomy and a sense of discipline, aim for fairness but develop respect for self and respect for others. They communicate their views as to standards and expectations of where and how they want the child to grow but recognize the child's individuals interests and special ways.

Table 2.1 lists some items from a scale developed by Clyde Robinson and his colleagues[2] to evaluate which combination of parenting types you might be. The whole scale is long to replicate here, so try the example items in the table to rate yourself (or your parent or your partner), as this will help explain the three types of parenting. The aim is to gain a sense of the three forms of parenting rather than to

TABLE 2.1 Authoritative (reasoning and listening) parenting items

WARMTH & INVOLVEMENT	NEVER	ONCE IN A WHILE	HALF THE TIME	VERY OFTEN	ALWAYS
Aware of problems or concerns about child in school	1	2	3	4	5
Gives comfort and under-standing when child is upset	1	2	3	4	5
Encourages child to talk about the child's troubles	1	2	3	4	5
Reasoning/induction					
Explains the consequences of the child's behavior	1	2	3	4	5
Explains how we feel about his/her good and bad behavior	1	2	3	4	5
Talks it over and reasons with child when the child misbehaves	1	2	3	4	5
Democratic participation					
Considers child's preferences in making family plans	1	2	3	4	5
Allows child to give input into family rules	1	2	3	4	5
Takes child's desires into account before asking the child to do something	1	2	3	4	5
Good natured/easy going					
Is easy going and relaxed with child	1	2	3	4	5
Shows patience with child	1	2	3	4	5
Jokes and plays with child	1	2	3	4	5
Permissive parenting items					
Permissive follow through					
Threatens child with punish-ment more often than giving it	1	2	3	4	5
Gives in when child causes a commotion about something	1	2	3	4	5
Bribes child with rewards to bring about compliance	1	2	3	4	5

WARMTH & INVOLVEMENT	NEVER	ONCE IN A WHILE	HALF THE TIME	VERY OFTEN	ALWAYS
Ignoring misbehavior					
Allows child to interrupt others	1	2	3	4	5
Allows child to annoy someone else	1	2	3	4	5
Ignores child's misbehavior	1	2	3	4	5
Self-confidence					
Appears unsure on how to solve child's misbehavior	1	2	3	4	5
Finds it difficult to discipline child	1	2	3	4	5
Is afraid that disciplining child for misbehavior will cause the					
child to not like his/her parents	1	2	3	4	5
Authoritarian parenting items					
Verbal hostility					
Explodes in anger towards child	1	2	3	4	5
Argues with child	1	2	3	4	5
Yells or shouts when child misbehaviors	1	2	3	4	5
Corporal punishment					
Uses physical punishment as a way of disciplining a child	1	2	3	4	5
Grabs child when being disobedient	1	2	3	4	5
Guides child by punishment more than by reason	1	2	3	4	5
Non-reasoning, punitive strategies					
Punishes by taking privileges away from a child with little if any explanations	1	2	3	4	5
Punishes by putting child off somewhere alone with little if any explanations	1	2	3	4	5
Uses threats as punishment with little or no justification	1	2	3	4	5

(*Continued*)

TABLE 2.1 (Continued)

WARMTH & INVOLVEMENT	NEVER	ONCE IN A WHILE	HALF THE TIME	VERY OFTEN	ALWAYS
Defectiveness					
Demands that child does things	1	2	3	4	5
Scolds and criticizes to make child improve	1	2	3	4	5
Scolds or criticizes when child's behavior doesn't meet expectations	1	2	3	4	5

definitively classify yourself (you would need the whole scale of 133 items to do this reliably).

To calculate the authoritative/reasonable score, add your responses from the Reasoning and Listening parenting items and divide by 12 (the number of items). For the permissive score, add the scores for the permissive items and divide by 9. For the authoritarian score, add the scores for the authoritarian items and divide by 12. Now you should have three scores between 1 and 5. This will indicate which one of the three you are highest in and which one is the lowest. Your score in each of the three relates to the anchors in the scale (1 = Never, 2 = Once in a while, 3 = Half the time, 4 = Very often, and 5 = Always). Remember, these questions are only part of the total scale, so the result is indicative but not highly reliable. But completing the partial scale will add to your understanding of the three parenting types.

The reasonable authoritative parent – the listener

There is plenty of evidence supporting the positive influence of reasoning and listening parenting. But being reasoning and listening alone is not enough. More is needed. What's missing is the **CONTENT** of reasoning and listening parents, that is, making reasonable demands and being highly responsive to your children; and this content relates to the development of your child's self-determination.

Go back and reread the description of reasoning and listening parenting. It is absent any content, any context, any direction, and any outcomes. It argues for autonomy, fairness, reasoning, soliciting objections, outlining standards and expectations – but about what! Our argument is that there are desirable outcomes that these all need to be directed toward. Of course, some of you will have different outcomes to ours, and they certainly are likely to differ across cultures (e.g., in many Eastern countries there is a notion of 'pride in family' that is less evident in Western countries – and hence the Tiger Mom mantra that aims that their children show the pride of their families, do not let the family down in public, and are motivated to do well (by whosever standards) so as to not let the family down.

The Tiger Mum phenomenon derives from the principle of 'guan' or training that emphasizes the importance of obedience and self-discipline. Hence, the outcome for the parent is to develop these attributes. Recall the Confucian virtues: loyalty, family piety, righteousness, benevolence, affection, trustworthiness, harmony, and peace. The Tiger Mom emphasizes the first three, sometimes to the detriment of the last five. Why wait, why not aim for all eight at any age and not be so overzealous and set too high expectations?

Listening is a major attribute of the reasoning and listening parent. I (JH) first encountered Carl Rogers, during my graduate class, when we watched a video of Carl Rogers, Fritz Perls, and Albert Ellis conducting a counseling session with the same client.[3] We were then asked to delve deeper into each, and I remain impressed with the rigor of Rogers as an experimentalist as well as a psychotherapist. One of his powerful claims was that it was essential to start interactions with clients with 'reflective listening' – which became (wrongly) clichéd as 'Um, tell me more' and parroting back the client's words. The listening developed by Rogers was more demonstrating to the client that the therapist was listening, respecting (but not necessarily agreeing), and demonstrating genuineness.[4] Then there are moves to go beyond this empathetic connection to testing understandings and see how the client reacts to life situations, allowing the client to amend or reject the therapist's interpretations of what they mean, how they react or not, and their coping strategies but with much care not to jump to impulsive interpretations.

Similarly, for the parent (and even more powerful when these skills are taught to your child), this does not mean the parent shows a blank screen, but via this empathetic listening they begin building a positive relation, establishing trust and understanding, and model to the children the skills of empathetic listening, all leading to later working with the child on goals (the more the goals are proscribed then the less likely the child will adopt them). By checking your understanding of what you are hearing, the parent is asking – Is what I am saying now precisely accurate for you? And if not, help me revise my understanding – thus pulling the child into a discussion what they are actually experiencing, and allowing the parent to demonstrate that they can stand in the other's shoes and see how they construct their world (of course, not necessarily agreeing with it). This is far from reflection in the sense of retelling what they hear, it is reflection more in terms of allowing the child to hear themselves, hear the emotional essence of what they have expressed, and hear another's interpretation of what they are hearing, as so often what we say is not what we mean so empathetic listening is a powerful way of the client realizing how to better express what they mean.

Parenting is far from all listening, as there comes a time, when the dialogue focus needs to change from the child to the parent, to take the role of talking and helping the child listen to what they have said, what they have heard, articulating their interpretations, the accuracy of what we said, and then seeing the world from the parents' point of view. We listen to feedback, for values, for conflict, to welcome discussion about their ways of thinking, hearing their errors and logic, we can listen for, listen out, listen to, listen in, and most important listening allows us to be open to difference, to understanding, and to demonstrating respect for having listened.

John Medina advocates three basic rules for teaching these 'reasonable and listening' skills: clear and consistent rules, rules that are explained, and swift negative reinforcement (not to be confused with punishment).[5] Negative reinforcement leads to strengthened desirable behaviors whereas punishment tends to weaken them – he provides a great example:

> As a child you probably discovered that when you burn your finger, cold water provides immediate pain relief, removing the obnoxious experience. When a response pays off, it tends to get repeated. The next time you get a burn – an aversive stimulus – the probability multiplies of you running to the nearest sink. This is negative reinforcement because your response was strengthened by the removal (or avoidance) of aversive stimuli. It's different from positive reinforcement, which is when an action leads to such a wonderful experience, you want to repeat the action.
>
> (p. 238)

2 The importance of developing self-determination

Developing a child's self-determination requires a gradual release of responsibility for learning to the child from the parent and there are deliberate skills in this gradual release. The aim is to develop individual autonomy in later life – and this means more direction to teach the skills of self-determination through the child's life. Sometimes, providing autonomy to make decisions can lead to conflict between the child's use of this autonomy and your desire as to what they should do with this autonomy, hence, the importance of developing your own and your child's coping strategies for dealing with conflict.

Self-determination theory is one of the most well-supported theories in psychology. Developed by Edward Deci and Richard Ryan,[6] it has three major parts – autonomy, relatedness, and competence. These three components work together to form our sense as a person and underlie human motivation and sense of success. The three components are what reasoning and listening parents need to foster in their children and within their families (and for themselves as parents):

- The need for *autonomy* is met when the child feels that their actions are their own.
- The need for *competence* is met when the child feels the task before them is within their skill set, and they have some control or predictability over their environment.
- The need for *relatedness* is met when a child is attached and accepted by a community, group, or family.

When these three needs are supported by parents, teachers, and others around a child, then the child's motivation, psychological well-being and academic outcomes are likely to be optimally supported.

3 The need to develop coping strategies

While on a trip to the playground Emma was doing her usual: throwing herself as fast as she can down the slide, flying off the end and then running straight back up. When she was running up the stairs toward the slide, she missed a step and tripped. No harm done thought her mum. The metal platform made it sound worse than it was. But Emma is not up yet. She is wondering what to do here, she has clearly experienced a fright but is not hurt. Her mum waits for a second; here it comes, she thinks.

Emma's face turns from a confused look of what happened to a 'MY WHOLE WORLD IS ENDING' face. Emma is now screaming and running toward her mum saying that she has hurt herself. Now in the loving embrace of Mum, she is still crying and being unreasonable and clearly not hurt. She is more embarrassed that she fell than anything. What does Mum do? How does Mum react to the Mum crying over a little 'booboo'?

She provides comfort and acknowledgment that Emma has hurt herself. She says, 'Oh no, are you okay?'. Don't worry, here you go', and she puts a bandage over the part that hurts; Emma is now all better, happy, and off playing again, a bit slower but still happy. The 'magic bandage' has worked. But wait, why a bandage? Emma was not cut or bleeding. She just slipped and clearly overreacted (which is totally normal for a 3-year-old), so what did that bandage do? It acted as a coping strategy. Emma knows that you put bandages on cuts, and cuts hurt. But has her mum dealt with what happened, or has she masked a lack of resilience with a bandage? Either way Emma has overcome the pain because the magic bandage has taken the pain away. But what about next time when Emma trips?

Using a cover or a quick fix to mask or solve a situation that does not require talking is just that, a quick fix. It's not a solution. In this situation, the quick fix was all that was needed. Emma was able to recover and keep playing happily.

Developing skills to reconnect the emotional part of the brain with the logical part – being able to shift from panic mode back to logic mode is important for developing resilience and the ability to deal with situations. The mum has done nothing wrong here, but she allowed the quick fix and ignored the fact that Emma was in the emotional flight mode. If the mum had taken a different approach and talked through what happened, she would have allowed Emma to work through what happened. 'Yes I fell, yes it hurt for a bit, yes I got more of a fright than anything.' This would have allowed Emma to realize 'I am not hurt and I need to slow down a bit and think about what I am doing so that I don't fall again'. So next time Emma has that confused 'what just happened' face, she will know how to react with better outcomes for all. How we approach these situations and how we talk about them allow these coping strategies to build and become stronger.

Note that being a reasonable parent becomes more critical in times of stress. 'Stress' is another notion that has changed in how we understand it over the past decades. Since the pioneering work by Richard Lazarus and Susan Folkman[7] in the 1980s, the stress literature has moved from debates about stress to debates about coping with stress. During COVID we hear many claims about the stress on children, and we read the headlines such as '80% of parents are worried about their children's well-being'. Perhaps, instead of focusing on the 80%, the key is to ask why the other 20% do not also worry. It is not the worry or stress we should focus on but the coping strategies to deal with the worry and stress. As it turns out, children often have very resilient coping strategies in the face of stress, and if they don't, we need to teach the optimal strategies for coping.

Stress occurs when what we expect to happen does not happen as we expected and then exceeds our capacity to deal with these failed or thwarted expectations. Stress occurs when people confront situations that tax their ability to manage them and when they do not have appropriate coping strategies to react to the stress.

A critical role of parents is to build coping strategies – they cannot necessarily control the stress. Enveloping children in cotton wool is never a good parenting strategy. Coping aims to prevent or reduce threat, harm, and loss and thus reduce distress.

Richard Lazarus and Susan Folkman carefully distinguished between problem-focused and emotion-focused coping.

Problem-focused coping is directed at the stressor itself: taking steps to remove or to evade it or to diminish its impact if it cannot be evaded.

Emotion-focused coping is aimed at minimizing distress triggered by stressors. Because there are many ways to reduce distress, emotion-focused coping includes a wide range of responses, from self-soothing (e.g., ruminating on negative thoughts) to attempts to escape stressful situations (e.g., avoidance, denial, wishful thinking).

They were careful to note both types of coping can occur simultaneously. For example, effective emotion-focused coping can diminish negative distress, making it possible to consider the problem more calmly, perhaps yielding better problem-focused coping. Take the reaction Tiger Woods has to a bad shot – he allows himself to count to five and emote and permit negative criticisms of himself. On the count of five, his problem-solving takes over as he realizes the shot cannot be replayed, and he moves on with a fresh(er) mind to the next shot.

This strategy is used a lot in our sports coaching. When the player drops a catch, for example, we allow the player to emote until the count of five, but then on five, the player comes back to the team, who support each other and move on. Otherwise, the negative emotion and reaction can be stored up and lead to problems later.

There are many problem-focused coping strategies:

a *Engagement* versus *disengagement* strategies. The parent can deal with the stressful situation (engagement) or remove themselves (disengagement) and focus on the reaction to the stress (usually the emotions). Love the sinner, hate the sin! You can problem-solve, strategize, plan, and adjust your actions and reactions.

b The parent can *rethink* the situation (cognitive restructuring), reduce their expectations, or try again (preferably with a different strategy of attack). You can seek information, read, observe, ask others, seek help.

c The parent can be *meaning-focused*, which involves seeing the learning benefits of stressful situations, finding benefits in adversity, and restructuring the situation to be less negative. You can be self-reliant, express emotions, protect yourself from others, and regulate how you feel and act.

d The parent can be *proactive* and realize that it may be hard to meet the challenge *and seek resources* to help them (or remove themselves from the task). Many students do not invest in learning because they realize that such investment is unlikely to lead to success, so why should they bother. You can seek comfort, help, social assurance, and use all resources around you.

Emotion-focused coping can involve changing focus (looking at something else), planning and deliberately seeking distracting activities, using the emotional reaction as a flight path from the challenge, venting, and feeling helpless. Table 2.2 outlines some of these emotion-focused coping strategies, and their reorientation to more problem-focused strategies.

Understanding coping invokes the concept of challenge. When adults or children take on tasks, they can be challenged in good ways (hope, eagerness, excitement) or be rebuffed in meeting these

TABLE 2.2 Various emotion-focused coping strategies, their symptoms, and more positive solutions

EMOTION-FOCUSED COPING	SYMPTOMS	POSITIVE SOLUTIONS
Accommodation	Distraction, cognitive restructuring, minimization	Adjust reactions
Negotiation	Bargaining, persuasion, priority setting	Find new options
Helplessness	Confusion cognitive exhaustion	Reach limits of action
Escape	Avoidance, withdrawal, denial	Remove from the situation
Delegation	Complaining, whining, self-pity	Find limits
Social isolation	Social withdrawal, concealment, avoiding others	Withdraw
Submission	Giving in, moving away	Give up challenge
Oppositional	Other blame, projection aggression	Remove constraints

challenges (negative reactions are often then experienced). Or they can set the bar so close to where they are now and not only not be challenged but also not grow; rather, they learn to be scared of the world, which is full of challenges, and develop emotion-focused coping strategies to buttress them from this scary world. A critical role of parenting is to teach their children optimal coping strategies to react to challenges.

Children also develop different coping strategies at different ages. Problem-solving in the early years (0–2 years) may involve more repetition, practice, and effort, between 2–5 years children may learn to cope by asking for help, and from age 6 on, they may do more strategizing and planning. Children are more likely to seek social in the elementary years and by the teenage years are expected to be more self-reliant – at least in how they react to stressors. As they get older, they will use more problem-solving strategies such as reframing or restructuring a problem situation, using self-talk to calm negative emotions, and generating alternative solutions to solve problems.

Many families have a dominant reaction to stressful situations. For some, their 'go to' reaction may be to minimize the stressor ('it's not a big deal', 'get over it'); some just worry; some vent and rant or resort to verbal aggression (e.g., they take it out on others); some see the failure as a chance to renegotiate, try again, or seek help; and some restructure the challenge as not worth aiming for or lower the priority or the bar for success in the challenge. Whatever the coping strategy, it is how parents teach their children to react in these adverse, stressful situations that can lead to the greatest subsequent effects on children's learning at school.

Failure can lead to stress. Kyle Haimovitz and Carol Dweck (2016) investigated parents who viewed failure as debilitating compared to those who see failure as enhancing. The title sums up the main message: 'Parents' Views of Failure Predict Children's Fixed and Growth Intelligence Mindsets'. They claim that parents who believe that failure is an enhancing experience that facilitates learning and growth (a failure-is-enhancing mindset) have long-term positive benefits on their children compared to parents who believe that failure is a debilitating experience that inhibits learning and productivity (a failure-is-debilitating mindset). The latter exhibit to their children more anxiety, are more focused on the outcomes than the how to learn and improve, and send messages that ability is fixed and not changeable.

They asked the parents questions about whether

1 the effects of failure are positive and should be utilized,
2 experiencing failure facilitates learning and growth,
3 experiencing failure enhances performance and productivity,
4 experiencing failure inhibits learning and growth,
5 experiencing failure debilitates performance and productivity, and
6 the effects of failure are negative and should be avoided.

Failure mindsets are visible to children from a very young age. Haimovitz and Dweck state that parents who view failure as enhancing 'approach their children's performance with a focus on how to learn and improve, with less worry about setbacks and what they might mean about their children' (p. 860), whereas the more parents believed that failure was debilitating, the more likely their children were to see their parents as concerned with their performance outcomes and grades rather than their learning and improvement. This is because these parents react to their children's failures by focusing more on their children's ability or performance than on their learning.

John Gottman talks a lot about emotional coping.[8] This involves empathizing with the child (i.e., seeing the world through the child's eyes) and actively teaching children how to cope with negative feelings. Thus, parents should not dismiss the feelings nor be accepting and warm but leave their child to work out themselves how to cope. There are five steps of emotion coaching:

1 Be aware of your child's emotion
2 Recognize your child's expression of emotion as a perfect moment for intimacy and teaching
3 Listen with empathy and validate your child's feelings
4 Help your child learn to label their emotions with words
5 Set limits when you are helping your child to solve problems or deal with upsetting situations appropriately

When Gottman followed a group of students from ages 5–8, those 5-year-olds whose parents used emotional coping steps (on each other and with their children) had higher school achievement and fewer behavioral problems. They were also more able to inhibit impulsive responses and were physically healthier. One important reason for this finding is that within families where emotions are recognized and emotional coping is developed, this leads to useful and appreciated language and skills for new situations, whereas in families where emotions are ignored, denied, or not seen as learning opportunities, there is little learning for new emotional situations.

Concluding comments

The major messages are how you can build trust, be seen as reliable, and show a high level of confidence and respect for your child. This involves being seen as reasonable and highly responsive to your child. Stand in their shoes and see yourself; you are the adult and can do this whereas they may struggle to see the world through your eyes. The aim is to develop your child's sense of autonomy, skills in relating, and build their competence to interpret and react to their world – what is often termed *self-determination*.

A key set of skills is to develop your child's coping strategies, particularly so that they can cope with unexpected, unsuccessful, or failed or thwarted expectations. Coping aims to prevent or reduce threat, harm, and loss and thus reduce distress. Show your child that you are a listener, and are there to work with them in times of stress, mistakes, and failure.

Notes

1 Pinquart, M. (2017). Associations of parenting dimensions and styles with externalizing problems of children and adolescents: An updated meta-analysis. *Developmental Psychology, 53*(5), 873–932. Pinquart, M. (2017). Associations of parenting dimensions and styles with internalizing symptoms in children and adolescents: A meta-analysis. *Marriage & Family Review, 53*(7), 613–640. Pinquart, M. (2016). Associations of parenting styles and dimensions with academic achievement in children and adolescents: A meta-analysis. *Educational Psychology Review, 28*(3), 475–493.
2 Robinson, C., Mandleco, B., Olsen, S. F., & Hart, C. H. (1995). Authoritative, authoritarian, and permissive parenting practices: Development of a new measure. *Psychological Reports, 7*(7), 819–830.
3 Shostrom, E. L. (1965). *Three approaches to psychotherapy* [Film]. Psychological Films. Burry, P. J. (2008). *Living with the "The Gloria Films": A daughter's memory.* Ross-on-Wye.
4 Rogers, C. R. (1951). *Client-centered therapy: Its current practice, implications and theory.* Houghton Mifflin.
5 Medina, J. (2014). *Brain rules: 12 principles for surviving and thriving at work, home, and school.* Pear Press.
6 Ryan, R. M., & Deci, E. L. (2017). *Self-determination theory: Basic psychological needs in motivation, development, and wellness.* Guilford Press.
7 Lazarus, R. S., & Folkman, S. (1984). *Stress, appraisal, and coping.* Springer.
8 www.gottman.com/parents/

3

I am not alone

1 *The child is brought up in a village – now a huge village*

- Children differ in so many ways and will live in many communities.
- Children need to be taught to present, interpret, and interact in different contexts.

2 *The power of others – siblings, friends, bullies*

- Children within the same family experience their families very differently.
- Children grow in relation to others, from their experiences, from their learned reactions about how others react, and from their developing theories about how their world works.
- From others, they learn about conflict and develop coping strategies. Children need to be taught to develop the perspective of others (particularly in disputes).
- Friendship grows from shared activities, imitation, and the emerging notion of reciprocity.

3 *Teenagers want to be with their friends more than with their parents*

- Teenagers aim to build their reputations (how they want others to see them) and have their reputations endorsed by their peers.
- Be aware when a teenager does not have a reputation, as at this age, this is often a cause of loneliness.
- Peer groups play a fundamental role in the initiation and development of social reputations during adolescence and exert a great deal of control over the type of reputation an individual chooses, along with the behaviors in which they engage.

DOI: 10.4324/9781003257028-4

This chapter highlights the power of others – you are far from alone in parenting as your child is far from alone in growing up. As adults, we experience other family members, friends, and bullies as do your children, and being and working with others are major buffers from loneliness, major teachers of skills and attitudes, and keys to developing social sensitivity.

I (Kyle) grew up in the '90s in the US and a memory that has stuck with me was the times when I spent watching television with Mum and Dad. I did not get a choice of what we were watching as these times were rare – as Mum was doing her PhD and any time away from a book or computer was precious to her and Dad, who traveled like crazy and just enjoyed sitting with Mum and his kids. I cherished this quiet time with both my parents. But what mum wanted to watch was Full House. You would all remember this highly popular television series, which aired between 1987–1995. Full House was based on a widowed broadcaster who needed help to raise his three daughters: Danny Tanner, played by Bob Saget; his Elvis-obsessed brother-in-law Jesse, played by John Stamos; and his childhood best friend Joey, a comedian.

Throughout the series there are many different people who are in the lives of the three young girls. But they all have the same goal, the welfare and raising of the girls. It was a very unlikely and unqualified trio, but their difference provided a solid base where there was much laughter, listening, and learning.

It was not the household that the family had wished for, but it was a household of love, caring, fun, and routine. As parents we can learn a lot from Full House and others like it.

Over the years there have been many examples of groups of people influencing a child's life, and what do they all tell us? That the roles of others play an important part in a child's life. These examples on television are based on difficult or unexpected circumstances, but more commonly you have the role of brothers, uncles, aunties, grandparents, and, if you are lucky enough, great-grandparents. A nanny or an au pair also has a part to play in raising a child. These people who are in our lives all help shape us into who we become, each playing a different role and providing experiences and caring that we may not get otherwise.

1 The child is brought up in a village – now a huge village

In the previous chapter, we spoke about how siblings can be quite different from each other, although they are brought up in families by the same parents. Children have different potentials, different realizations of their lives, and different experiences. And, through multiple interactions with others, they often have different views on the world. Everyone in the family brings their personal resources, conceptualized as skill (e.g., knowledge), will (dispositions), and thrill (motivations), which we talk about in Mind frame 4.

Not every child, no matter how perfect their upbringing, will be an Einstein, a Madame Curie, a Mother Teresa, or a Martin Luther King. No matter those who proclaim 'bring me a child until they are 7, and I will make them what you want' – this is unlikely to happen in today's world, especially if the 'what you want' is intellectual brilliance. The older insulated world of the closed family is now battered by the outside influences available within the home. Tara Westover wrote about her experiences in such a closed family, and *Educated* is a powerful message about the resourcefulness of kids to break out of these closets.

We are not returning here to the barren debate about 'heredity or environment' as the more important influence. Jim Flynn sums up the issue nicely.[1] He asks, imagine a child who is born a little taller and quicker than average: 'They may perhaps enjoy playground basketball more and play more, so already they're upgrading their environment in terms of enriched basketball practice. And then, when they get to school, the grade school coach may see them and say '"Hey, they're worth putting on the team."' And that, of course, upgrades their performance advantage more, and then they may make their high school team and get really good coaching'. Such small genetic advantages can turn into large performance advantages through these feedback loops. A parent's role is to magnify the potentials of their children by providing opportunities to learn, seek, and listen to feedback. The dilemma is to know these small advantages and this means parents need to be supportive when their children choose many different sports, activities, and experiences. With my (JH) boys, they tried every sport available, and it was not until a mid-teenager that Kyle settled on underwater hockey – going on to win a gold medal at the World Championships 2006 in Sheffield UK (www.uwhworlds2006

.net/). It is the perfect sport for a parent, as you cannot see the game, no point in cheering, there are no hassles between parents and referees, and you can sit in the stands and read your book with no guilt (see https://en.wikipedia.org/wiki/Underwater_hockey).

Children bring their own bundle of attributes – their own strengths and world views – into the family. But parents, in their socializing role, help realize, modify, and enhance a child's attributes, as do teachers, friends, media, and so many others. Children are more likely to learn at home to behave at home, to learn at school to behave at school, and to learn within friends to behave with friends. They quickly learn to 'code-switch' – that is, learn the codes of different settings – and pity if they do not as therein lie a major source of conflict. The child is the same person, but they need to be taught to present, interpret, and interact in different contexts.

2 The power of others – siblings, friends, bullies

Children within the same family experience their families very differently. Each child experiences different interactions, and their parents, siblings, and friends are seen through their individual lens – and these all combine in interesting ways to create a different environment for each child within the same family.

It is worth noting that siblings can differ from each other as much as any two random children. For example, Sandra Scarr noted that the IQ difference between siblings is about 12–13 points, and between any two randomly chosen people in the population the difference is only 18 IQ points.[2] Thus, siblings can differ from each other only slightly less in IQ than any two random children differ. Scarr also showed that for personality, interest, attitudes, and psychopathology, siblings are as different as random pairs of children. So, differences are among the children in your family can be as different as any two children.

The key is how siblings interact with and develop each other – for better or for worse. They talk, listen, share emotions, demonstrate coping strategies to stress, engage in shared pretend, and develop their understanding of the world together. From age 2 on, a warm conversational relationship with other siblings (particularly older ones) can dramatically increase social understanding and develop language. They learn how to interact with others, how to share (or not), how to react to anger and stress, and how to cope with parents. By age 4, the child with an older sibling is exposed to over twice the amount of cognitive talk – that is, they talk about thinking, remembering, and knowing much more than a 4-year-old without a sibling. Yes, they can gain this from older friends at pre-school, but still, the child with an older sibling is advantaged. Contrary to the claims about firstborns being advantaged, there is much to gain from not being the firstborn (both JH and KH are second-borns).

When family environments are more stressful, siblings tend to show greater differences to each other – which again shows the differences that each child can have in their functioning within a family. When a child forms friends this can affect siblings by increasing jealousy or decreasing closeness. Not all children have positive relationships with siblings, and this is where bullying often starts: Those bullied at home are more likely to be bullied at school and have adjustment problems.[3]

Children grow in relation to others, from their experiences, from their learned reactions about how others react, and from their developing theories about how their world works. They can have low persistence (give up easily), be highly active, and express emotions strongly (e.g., frustration, anger, sadness). They can have high persistence (keep trying), show medium activity, and express their emotions strongly (e.g., joy, happiness, curiosity). Or they can be any other combination. But each sibling can develop differently, even in the same family structure and environment.

As we noted earlier, any little differences early on can slowly magnify. For example, children who exhibit negative moods can become more withdrawn over time, those who exhibit emotional intensity can become more dependent on adults, children who exhibit more trust can become more adventurous. Any lack of 'fit' between siblings can lead to them to criticize each other, overcompensate for the temperaments of other siblings, or cause disharmony among the siblings. This is why parents may need to intervene, in particular by encouraging the development of self-regulation and teaching the child the skills of becoming their own teacher. These skills enable the child to reflect on the effect they have on others (which we return to later), which, in turn, can help them accommodate differences, teach them code-switching (learning how to act and talk depending on the situation), help them know when to ignore what's happening, and when and how to fix conflicts.

These skills of the child becoming their own teacher can also help buffer against parental conflict as the child tries to make sense of the world. When the conflict, however, is focused on the child, this becomes difficult, given the power differential. You will surely have seen your 2-year-old become distressed or aggressive when you have a conflict – this is their way of deflecting the attention from your conflict.

When there is a conflict in the family, parents who continually intervene to resolve children's disputes can miss opportunities to teach their children the skills to resolve issues for themselves. But if there is little to no parental involvement, then older siblings are likely to dominate their younger siblings to ensure the rules (as they see them) are followed.

A clue to successful sibling relations is whether your child develops the perspective of others in these disputes – that is, develop empathy. When they have empathy, they can better understand the world of their brothers and sisters (but not necessarily agree with them), develop more effective ways to have their views considered, and be more likely to treat others more fairly. 'Fairness' is always high on what children desire from parents, siblings, and teachers. As parents, it is also wise to address the sin not the sinner in these situations. Remember, they are watching you and will often copy your methods of dealing with tensions when they are interacting with a sibling – negative begets negative, reasoning begets reasoning, listening begets listening, acceptance and fair play begets acceptance and fair play. This does NOT mean over-telling but adopting a set of fair boundaries and establishing what it means to be 'normal' in this family.

Siblings seem to be more important in early adolescence (12–14 years) when having a brother or sister is seen as important for companionship, trust, and intimacy and particularly important for navigating new adolescent challenges and moving away from parent oversight (Oliva & Arran, 2005). Siblings can also be important in times of negative life events (death, divorce, foster care placement, major sickness in the family) and in handling bullying.

Everyone knows the backseat-of-the-car rivalry of siblings. It is not low levels of sibling warmth and love that are the issue here but rather the opposite – the closeness of the siblings; there can be a lot of learning in this conflict. As noted in Chapter 2, it is building the coping strategies to deal with conflict that matters and which should be the focus of attention when the inevitable conflict arises. Teaching children to state their position, to see the world from the other's perspective, to continue to argue without resorting to tears and emotional venting, and to give and take are all important coping strategies. As with many other conflict situations (bullying, watching parents fight), it is not the conflict but the coping strategies that matter.

Separating, punishing, threatening, and ignoring are relatively ineffective. Collaborative problem-solving, which too rarely occurs, was endorsed most by children and parents as linked with the most positive outcomes.[4]

By the teen years, sharing possessions, deciding on who 'owns' what, and hurting, embarrassing, or humiliation become more common sources of sibling conflict and once again the skills of conflict coping, developing empathy to the others' views (they do not have to agree, just appreciate the alternative view), and firm mediation are key skills – by the teenagers and by their parents. Having parents show negative emotions can lead to teens imitating this reaction to conflict.

Having friends becomes more and more important as the child grows. A sense of belonging is essential for a child's well-being – something which is often overlooked. Consider, for example, that one of the best predictors of how well a child copes with a change of school or class is whether they make a friend in the first month.[5] Of course, friends can change often, especially in preteen years, but the presence of friends is critical. As parents, you cannot create friends for your children, but you can encourage friends' presence at play opportunities and, constructively, through social media, and you can be supportive of discussions about friends. During the teenage years, friends are crucial (more on this later).

In the early years, friendship grows from shared activities, imitation, and the emerging notions of reciprocity. As the child starts to become aware of the other as a resource (12–18 months), there is a shift from a focus on activities to a focus on the social relationship itself. Children can participate in rituals, games, and shared activities, and from this peer interaction, friendships develop – although friendship is not quite the right concept at this stage as the child is still self-centered. It is when verbal development and social pretend and fantasy play occur that the patterns of friendship become greater, as the child learns about the safety, fairness, and predictability of being with others. As learning increases, they realize that the other can enhance their own interactions. The joint organization of play begins at about 2.5–3 years, and then there can be assignments of roles in play and increased shared meaning of the activity and enjoyment.

These early friendships, although not always lasting, are the basis for learning the skills of interacting with others, how to participate in the give-and-take of friendships, and how to increase prosocial skills in the presence of others.

But, of course, there can be conflict. This is normal – it is the reaction to conflict that matters. Learning how to negotiate, resolve disputes, not feel hurt and isolated, and resist – these are the opportunities to learn how to socially interact and maintain friendships. As language develops, the child acquires more skills to deal with these conflicts. In any friendship there can be acceptance and rejection, shades in between, and changes over time. It is less about popularity but more about whether the other(s) accept the child for what they are and the child can contribute to the friendship. Friends can be supportive and they can disappoint, and that 'this is normal' is the message you need to convey to your children. The same coping strategies discussed earlier matter most with building and maintaining friendships.

Nearly every child, at some stage, is bullied, and this is very hard for parents, as they often have little power or any sense of control. Hugging and listening never seem enough, and dealing with bullied children is awful. We have been there. Bullying is common, sometimes brief, sometimes extended, sometimes quickly comes and goes, sometimes enduring. It can involve verbal belittling; being hit, slapped, and pushed; and being the subject of rumor-mongering, taunting, and gossip.

The nature of bullying can change from preschool to later childhood such that verbal aggression (insults, derogation, threats) gradually replaces direct physical aggression over this period.[6] Further, relative to early childhood, aggressive behavior in middle childhood is less instrumental (i.e., less directed toward possessing objects or occupying specific space) and more specifically hostile toward personal attributes. During early adolescence, there can be retaliatory aggression, relational bullying, gossip, and exclusion. During later elementary and in the high school years, being in peer groups becomes much more important, and appearing to 'do well' in front of peers becomes the prize. Gossip is usually among the 'in-group' about the 'out-group' or individuals. Not having a reputation to be esteemed becomes the fear of many adolescents.

The power of gossip can be nasty, particularly on social media. Gossip is in itself not bad – it can bring people closer together, it binds through sharing, it can be entertaining, and it can lead to desirable aspects of self-disclosure and self-expression. Gossip can enhance one's own self at the cost of others, it can be self-comparative in ways that help project and maintain a positive self-image, and it can help bond friendship groups, formed often on shared loyalty, self-disclosure, trust, and support. But when gossip is the mechanism of bullying, it can be vicious.

In a recent discussion with an experienced and wise school principal we asked him what was most different between his school now and six years ago. He commented that 'back then' there was much violence, fights in the playground, and bloodied noses. Today that has gone. Today the violence usually is not transparent until after the damage is done. I could fix bloodied noses, stop fights, had the powers to call the police, but bullying via social media eats at the soul, is rampant, is damaging before it is exposed, and can be so hard to stop. It crosses the border of school, home, and private lives – so who is responsible?

No wonder parents choose schools based on whom they want their child's friends to be.

No wonder bullying can be so painful.

Bullies admire power and wish to cultivate an image of their power. They want to be seen as strong, tough, and powerful and their bullying behaviors tend to occur where there is an audience. For many, bullying is a deliberate choice and a way to foster a reputation as a nonconforming and powerful figure. Bullies are motivated by the desire to enhance their reputation, whether their bullying is overt, covert, physical, or cyber in nature.

Robin Kowalski and colleagues[7] completed a meta-analysis of 131 studies of the correlates of cyberbullying. Children who are bullied face-to-face are also likely to be bullied online. Online bullies tend to have higher levels of anger, undertake risky online behavior, have high internet use, show moral disengagement, and are hyperactive. More important, factors that reduce bullying include providing a safe and positive school and home climate, listening, talking to your child about their online experiences and feelings, and having some degree of monitoring what's happening online. Note, though, that parental control of technology has a zero effect. It is not control; it is engaging with them about their online interactions. The effects of bullying on the victim do lead to marked decreases in achievement ($d = -0.33$).

Programs that had a positive impact on reducing bullying include those which included parents but didn't involve peers, involved cooperative group work, and used a whole-of-school approach.[8] Two of the more successful programs are KiVa (developed in Finland but widely used throughout the world) and the Olweus program.[9]

You can be proactive in helping your child discuss bullying, and the earlier you start, the better. Parents who are already having discussions with their children in safe, high-trust ways without negative consequences are better prepared for their children to discuss bullying – if such discussion is not already 'normal', it is much harder to start such a discussion in the home (particularly with teenagers). The responsive style of parenting is best (Mind frame 2) and authoritarian and laissez-faire approaches have the least positive impact on reducing bullying or on proactively reducing the impact on the bullied.

Look for signs such as your child starts using verbal or physical aggression to deal with conflict); starts talking about 'getting even'; shies away from talking about their emotions, particularly concerning friends; has low levels of skills in cooperative games or activities; and starts putting others down.

As a way to open up discussion about bullying with your child, have regular conversations about their social life at school, such as asking them what lunchtime is like at school or who they sit and play with at playtime. Ask them whether other kids call them names or push them, and ask how they respond. Start with general questions and move to more specific questions about bullying, but be careful, as this needs to be a conversation, not an interrogation. For a child to say they are being bullied can take some time. Use the same approach when asking about cyberbullying, ensure you talk regularly about their online activities, and ask about any unexpected reactions from their friends or strangers. Invite them to comment on what they would want to happen, what they would like you to do. Show them it is a safety issue, something you can deal with together. Avoid replicating bullying behavior in your response to the school, teachers, and others – this is the very behavior you want to stop, so you don't want to be modeling it.

Bullying is serious, so take it seriously and certainly do not minimize or excuse it. And these responsive reactions apply to the bullied and the bully. Get help early and talk to the school personnel, as you are the key to resolving any bullying of, or by, your child.

3 Teenagers want to be with their friends more than with their parents

Some years back, a group of us (Annemarie Carroll, Steve Houghton, Kevin Durkin, and JH) started a 20-year research program focused on adolescents in prison.[10] An aim was to understand (a) why adolescent crime decreased about age 17, (b) what was the causal mechanism to get into the crime and maintain the interest, and (c) why crime among adolescents was usually a group crime. We built a model based on 'reputation enhancement' that helps explain these three issues. It did not take us long to see how this model was applicable across the teenage years for most adolescents and that there were major problems for a large cohort of adolescents who did not have a reputation or a means to enhance their reputation.

First, note that during adolescence the world changes. Friends become more critical, and sometimes more important to development than parents. Ruth Harris[11] argued that in the formation of an adult, genes matter, peers matter, but parents don't matter. She argues that children come into the world already different from one another thanks to their genes, and parents treat their children differently precisely because of these early differences – which can become magnified as they grow up. Children soon learn that their behavior can be and is different in the presence of parents compared to when with others of their age – and therein lies the start of their powerful sense of self. Social comparison is a key part of discovering and finding yourself, regardless of what your friendships look like. The world that children share with their peer group is what shapes their behavior, modifies the characteristics they were born with, and determines the sort of people they will be when they grow up.

Harris argues that a child's goal is not to become a successful adult no more than a prisoner's goal is to become a successful guard. A child's goal is to be a successful child. Thus, the influence of peers is stronger than the influence of adults, and this is especially the case from about age 10 on. Within the peer group, the role of adults is minimized, and during adolescence it is minimal – particularly compared to the power of peers. For adolescents, quality time is time spent with peers more than with parents. Within peer groups, inequality reigns and dealing with this ebb and flow over the pushes and shoves, the love and denied friendships, can be critical learnings to survive in the adult world of inequality (not that she defends inequalities).

A group of researchers had adolescents indicate their activities, moods, and company at random intervals across a 1-week period.[12] Mihaly Csikszentmihalyi and Reed Larson calculated that during a typical week, even discounting time spent in classroom instruction, adolescents spend almost a third (29%) of their waking hours with peers. This is more than double the amount spent with parents and other adults (13%). Moreover, adolescent peer interaction takes place with less adult guidance and control than peer interaction in middle childhood. Adolescents love peer groups.

When Annemarie, Steve, Kevin, and JH studied what happened in the crime peer groups, we noted that the formation, binding, and continuing in these groups were little different from how other peer groups behaved – sports players, musicians, gifted children, clubs, and so on. It was a few years in when the obvious hit us in the face. While adolescents loved being in peer groups that enhanced their sense of reputation, many adolescents did not have a reputation in any domain or a peer group within which to be esteemed – here is where we saw the aloneness, the anomie, the despair, and the solitary use of drugs.

A 'reputation' is the estimation held about a person by others. The need for a reputation highlights the critical importance of the adolescent's peer group. This reputation needs to be appreciated through direct interactions among mutual acquaintances or more indirectly through gossip, rumor, social media, and other communications. Adolescents, in particular, recognize the importance of an audience for forming a reputation and indeed are acutely sensitive to this sense of social awareness. It allows them to present themselves in a particular way so that they are accredited with specific qualities of character.

Consider a dominant theme in school shooters – they often work in pairs and create a reputation between the two of them. When this reputation is not recognized by other peers, they can resort to violence to demonstrate that they indeed did deserve the reputation they had built for themselves.

AN APPLICATION TO SCHOOL SHOOTING[13]

Since 2000, there have been more than 300 deaths from school shootings in the US. The presence of guns, the publicity from each shooting, and the malaise and motives of the killers are all linked. Our research over the past 20 years, however, shows that there are further major underlying causes. Knowing and reacting to the underlying causes could prevent many mass shootings. So many adolescents have access to guns, are bullied, and want revenge but do **not** resort to killing their peers and teachers.

To prevent mass school shootings by teenagers it is important to understand the psyche of those who commit these murders. Common among the underlying causes is the killer's desire to enhance their reputation. This yearning for peer recognition and enhanced status is a common cause of adolescent crime and general behavior, from the gifted to athletes to class jokesters. For those who carry out mass school shootings, the visibility created by media coverage provides a vehicle for them to obtain the notoriety they crave.

Our two decades of research demonstrate the importance of reputation among peers as a key underlying mechanism for adolescents' goals and behavior. Traditionally, an immediate audience was essential to attain a reputation. The act needed to be directly witnessed by or communicated to others. However, the introduction and widespread use of social media now mean that a physical audience is not essential. School shooters gain instantaneous worldwide notoriety and, in some instances, adulation and copycats.

School shooters often work alone or in pairs, building up sets of beliefs about themselves – as warriors, as protectors, or as avengers of past wrongs. Rather than engaging with a range of friends, they secret themselves in a closed world and seek relief in violent computer games, chat sites, and online social networks. They often create and save manifestos on their computers, to be shared with the world after the event. They build a world where they have some control, and, most importantly, some recognition from peers for their beliefs.

Their high-level planning is often unemotional, purposeful, and lacking empathy for anyone in their way, and they perceive themselves as masculine and gutsy. In isolating themselves they are avoiding the attention of parents and teachers. In some cases, parents inadvertently provide resources by teaching them to shoot guns safely and for enjoyment or leaving them alone in their rooms to feed their belief system. Most school shooters come from families with legal guns.

They increasingly protect and safeguard their plans as the event comes closer, making it harder to detect. However, they often hint or leak the shooting event in anticipation of their enhanced reputation. Eventually, they execute the shooting in an attempt to show all their *peers that this reputation is deserved and should be recognized. In their barbarity they are screaming, 'See me, I am real, I am smart, I do have a manifesto, I can dominate and control others, and I should be respected. See me, I have extensively planned for this occasion and you now know I am seriously worth paying attention to'.*

Every teenager strives for a reputation, so everyone (fellow students, parents, teachers) needs to be aware of their attempts to enhance their status. You need to listen to them, ask about their friends, spend time with them, and learn how they wish to be esteemed. About a third of all teenagers struggle to get the peer recognition they seek, and this often leads to disengagement and the building of internal worlds to feed their reputations. Adolescent school shooters rarely have a history of drug abuse, violence, crime, or animal cruelty but often have grievances against at least one of their targets and aim for a very public rampage. They are often considered 'weird' or 'strange' by others, and this could be an early warning sign.

When a shooting has taken place, the media must also take responsibility with their reporting, ensuring they do not glorify or give kudos to the shooter through names, photographs, and continual coverage of the event – this includes not providing a growing tally of injured or dead (particularly as the number helps depersonalize the real people who have become victims). The media's current approach of reporting mass school shootings makes it clear that you cannot only become a household name and receive a reputation as a mass murderer, but you can also achieve notoriety. This is feeding the next teenager searching for a reputation among his peers.

Adolescents are major architects of their own reputations through how they build and present their desired self-image to others. Reputations play a central role in the lives of adolescents, whether in conformity, physical appearance, or transgression and crime. Peer groups play a fundamental role in the initiation and development of social reputations during adolescence and exert a great deal of control over the type of reputation an individual chooses, along with the behaviors in which they engage.

Enhancing and maintaining a reputation is vital to all adolescents. Equally important is the audience to whom these actions are visible, as well as the perceptions and descriptions of selves and others, which foster the person's self-image. For some adolescents, the deliberate choice of a reputation is a criterion for group membership, a means to impress peers and gain their approval. Moreover, it is a strategy of self-protection and redress for the individual and the group. Being aware of how adolescents wish to be presented to others is critical to understanding them. Knowing their friends (who often they do not want you to know) can help see how your adolescent is perceived.

Be prepared: To build and maintain their reputation, many adolescents select and accomplish very specific and challenging goals. This is how some gain a 'rep' and why they can embark on risky tasks – it is not unthinking behavior; it is impressing behavior – not to you but to those among whom they wish to have a reputation. And they want to establish a reputation that is separate from family, siblings, and home – which can cause heartache for parents. It is not a sign of a lack of love or gratitude, but rather, it is part of becoming an adolescent. It is important to establish a home life where you understand your adolescent's reputation, and you allow your adolescent to create and explore this sense of self in the family context.

Remember that for many adolescents, peer acceptance and parental acceptance are comfortably aligned whereas for others, parental rejection is part of the reputation. Pity the adolescent who does not have a sense of belonging in a peer group; loneliness can be a killer. Some adolescents do become loners – this can be painful, but sometimes being alone can be wonderful solitude. Adolescents go to great lengths to cultivate and protect their reputation of choice. By about age 16–18, love enters and couples grow together, and then the reputation enhancement by the group is far less important.

Concluding comments

You are not alone, there is a remarkable power in others, and developing your own and your children's friends is a major task of successful parenting. The world is so much easier to access and know about; your child will live and be asked to cope with many communities, and there are skills to be taught about making, keeping, and adjusting to new friendship groups. Loneliness is no fun particularly as they become teenagers, when having a reputation that is appreciated and enhanced by friends becomes all important.

Notes

1 Flynn, J. R. (2012). *Are we getting smarter?: Rising IQ in the twenty-first century*. Cambridge University Press.

2 Scarr, S., & Grajek, S. (1982). Similarities and differences among siblings. In M. E. Lamb & B. Sutton-Smith (Eds.), *Sibling relationships: Their nature and significance across the lifespan* (pp. 357–381). Erlbaum.

3 Wolke, D., & Samara, M. M. (2004). Bullied by siblings: Association with peer victimisation and behaviour problems in Israeli lower secondary school children. *Journal of Child Psychology and Psychiatry*, *45*(5), 1015–1029.

4 Kramer, L., Perozynski, L. A., & Chung, T. Y. (1999). Parental responses to sibling conflict: The effects of development and parent gender. *Child Development*, *70*(6), 1401–1414.

5 Galton, M., Morrison, I., & Pell, T. (2000). Transfer and transition in English schools: Reviewing the evidence. *International Journal of Educational Research*, *33*(4), 341–363.

6 Underwood, M. K., & Rosen, L. H. (2010). Gender and bullying: Moving beyond mean differences to consider conceptions of bullying, processes by which bullying unfolds, and cyberbullying. In D. L. Espelage & S. M. Sweare (Eds.), *Bullying in North American schools* (pp. 33–42). Routledge.

7 Kowalski, R. M., Giumetti, G. W., Schroeder, A. N., & Lattanner, M. R. (2014). Bullying in the digital age: A critical review and meta-analysis of cyberbullying research among youth. *Psychological Bulletin*, *140*(4), 1073.

8 Zych, I., Farrington, D. P., Llorent, V. J., & Ttofi, M. M. (2017). *Protecting children against bullying and its consequences* (pp. 5–22). Springer International Publishing.

9 http://violencepreventionworks.org/public/olweus_bullying_prevention_program.page

10 Carroll, A., Houghton, S., Durkin, K., & Hattie, J. A. (2009). *Adolescent reputations and risk: Developmental trajectories to delinquency*. Springer Science & Business Media.

11 Harris, J. R. (1998). *The nurture assumption: Why children turn out the way they do*. Free Press.

12 Csikszentmihalyi, M., & Larson, R. (1984). *Being adolescent*. Basic Books.

13 Carroll, A. M., Hattie, J. A. C., & Houghton, S. (2018). *School shootings are preventable: It begins with understanding reputation*. www.edweek.org/education/opinion-school-shootings-are-preventable-it-begins-with-understanding-reputation/2018/02

The foundations to develop learners

I develop my child's skill, will, and sense of thrill

1   *Developing the skill – working memory, executive functioning*

■   The driver of learning is executive functioning, which relates to how we think and how we process information. There are three major components: the skill to concentrate and avoid being distracted, the ability to shift between different tasks or across ideas, and the art of updating our thinking based on incoming information.

2   *Developing the will – confidence and a growth mindset*

■   Children develop their personality with us, because of us, despite us.

■   Their most critical personality attribute is developing self-confidence – the confidence to take on challenging tasks, the confidence to seek help, the confidence to work with others to achieve outcomes, the confidence to see themselves as learners, the confidence to seek and action feedback, and the confidence to enjoy the gift of failure.

3   *Developing the thrill – passion and investment*

■   Motivation relates to choosing to engage, act, or invest in actions.

■   Everyone has the fundamental need of feeling related, competent, and autonomous to develop and function optimally.

■   Children need to learn to master tasks and not merely to complete tasks because of factors (such as rewards) that are external to the joy, value, and positive learning from the task.

DOI: 10.4324/9781003257028-6

This chapter discusses the three core notions of learning – developing our child's skills, will, and thrill in learning. The child is not merely a function of what they inherit and are born with, but the brain continues to grow and changes in critical ways during their first 20 years. The aim is to develop the skills, the confidence to undertake challenging learning, and invest with passion in learning. High ideals but realizable.

> *Every parent of a school-aged child will have experienced what it was like to see the child as a student during the COVID-19 remote learning in 2020. Every parent likes to imagine their child at school as a well-behaved, motivated, and inquisitive learner who asks questions, tries hard, and challenges their thinking. But during this pandemic, parents were able to see their child as a student at home.*
>
> *I (KH) know from firsthand experience as a teacher that the image parents had of their children as students was a bit different from the reality. The biggest complaint received from parents during lockdown was that they wanted their children back at school because the children were not motivated or didn't try hard with their work the way they did at school.*
>
> *This was a hard reality to face for some parents, but with children forced into something new, scary, and confusing, parents were able to see how much self-regulation or capability to learn that their children had, and why it's so important to develop these skills. Self-regulation involves the ability to ask questions, invest in learning, and make mistakes without the fear of being seen as 'dumb'. During remote learning, the children who did well and made shifts were not necessarily the academically smart children. The ones who had a strong sense of self-regulation (and executive functioning) were the most successful. The message is that the skills of self-regulation (and executive functioning) need to be understood, valued, and taught both at home and at school.*

There were three boys in the Hattie clan and the variability among them is enormous. Sometimes you would wonder how they could be related when the differences were so great. There are whole mythologies about the differences between the first-born, the beauty of the second-born (both John and Kyle were middle children), and the benefits of being last. But the research, especially the meta-analyses, is clear: Birth-order effects are a mirage.[1] At best, the later-born are more unconventional and rebellious, but this is a small enough difference to warrant great care in assuming it is the case for your youngest child.

Each child develops their own skills, their ways of seeing the world, their motivations for investing their time and intellect, and their personalities. As noted earlier, they develop from an early age a 'theory of mind' or way of seeing the world; this view changes over time, but it certainly is unique. Understanding the child's ways of thinking and seeing the world is the first step in respecting your child, although this is not to say you have to agree with or accept their ways of thinking – that is why you are the parent.

This chapter outlines the importance of listening to and developing your child's voice and how they react to situations, failure, and success. It outlines the various attributes of the child that lead to each unique voice.

1 Developing the skill – working memory, executive functioning

We noted in Mind frame 1 the importance of very young children building their theory of their world and how this forms the basis of their interactions with you, their siblings, and their world. We want as parents to advance this 'theory of mind' as they grow and interact with new situations and dilemmas, and as they go to school and drastically expand their world views.

This theory of mind relates to the skills needed to not only interpret the world, to make sense of it, but also to how we react, think, and process information. Executive functioning relates to the ability to concentrate and not be distracted or act impulsively, the ability to shift between different tasks or across ideas, and the art of monitoring and updating incoming information for task relevance. The ability to concentrate relates to our working memory. George Miller wrote a famous article in 1956 called 'Seven Plus or Minus Two', arguing that most of us humans can only hold between five and nine things in our short-term memory at a time (later work showed it was more like four to seven), and this can put a brake on our learning.[2] The ability to shift across tasks, or flexible thinking, is our skill to adapt, change, or modify and consider others' beliefs without necessarily agreeing with them. The art of monitoring and updating is how we consider incoming information or new situations and update our current theory of the world or interpretations. These are all skills needed to function in families, engage in school-work, and work together with siblings and peers.

Most of us have many false beliefs, and we survive very well in our individual worlds. Imagine that I believe the Earth is the center of the universe and that the sun and planets rotate around the Earth – this does not change the reality of the Earth rotating around the sun and no one is negatively affected, although I might have difficulties if I started to learn astronomy. People have a lot of world views that do not correspond to reality, and they live very happily. It is when contrary evidence is placed in front of them that people feel awkward and fight back with their beliefs. People can be resistant to new ideas – but this is often the optimal learning opportunity.

I (JH) once used this image of the planets revolving around the sun (Figure 4.1). A Nobel physicist emailed me in great dudgeon, asking how I could be so ignorant of planetary motion, how come I perpetuated myths and misinformation, and requested I remove the picture immediately. I bet you have seen this diagram perhaps as part of learning the names and order of planets from the sun (or perhaps you used the mnemonic 'My very energetic mother just served us nine pizzas' or with the demise of Pluto as a planet 'My very energetic mother just served us nachos'). But the physicist is right, the diagram misrepresents the orbital paths, the relative closeness to each other and the sun, and builds an incorrect world view of planetary rotation. A lot of learning for children is like this – they have a world view, it is then shown to be incorrect, so they have to relearn. If the initial world view is retained, this can lead to major issues with accommodating new information.

This development of a theory of mind goes through major changes as the child grows, sometimes influenced by the developments in the brain, but mostly through parents' teaching, teaching from school, and interactions with peers, media, and other social interactions.

The aspects of brain development we want to emphasize relate to self-regulation and executive functioning. Self-regulation refers to the skills that give some level of control over learning. Executive functioning is about how you process information and how you manage yourself. Together they are the skills needed to make sense of the world and knowing how to learn and how to interact with others.

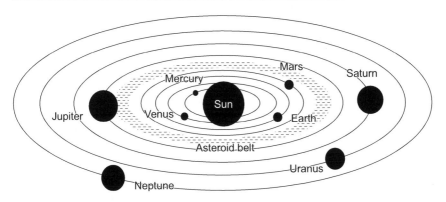

FIGURE 4.1 A common but misleading depiction of planetary rotation around the sun

There are many parts to self-regulation, including the following:

Flexibility	the ability to switch between ideas
Attention control	the ability to stay on task
Concept formation	how to relate ideas together
Error processing	how we react to errors
Working memory	how to store information in short-term memory

Self-regulation also relates to regulating emotions. For example, if someone does not have the cognitive resources to solve a problem, they may become frustrated, or they may become even more determined to solve it. Or they could get angry, or denigrate or attack others for putting them in this situation. You will surely have seen your kids express these emotions, and we are sure that as parents, you, like us, will have vented when you are stuck on a problem.

Self-regulation can also relate to how people interact with others to seek help (or not) to solve problems, to persevere, and to interpret the help others give them. It should be no surprise that helping your children develop self-regulation is one of the most critical things you can do to help your children learn.

Perhaps the greatest changes relate to this development of self-regulation. There are three major key learning skills, which are often couched in new jargon such as 'executive functioning', which helps children power their self-regulation. Executive functioning is mainly related to 'how' we think, or how we process information. It is the three major components of executive functioning – inhibition, task shifting, and monitoring and updating – that are most critical for parents to develop in the early years, as these components are the best predictors and causes of later learning. Note also they are 'content free' in that while they are important in learning the 3Rs (reading, writing, and 'rithmetic), they can and should be developed in a context more appropriate to young children (through play, listening to stories, and everyday interactions with parents and peers).

The first component, known as inhibition, is the ability to concentrate on the task at hand and avoid being distracted. This skill of not being easily distracted is a learned skill and does not occur in meaningful ways until the child is about 7 years old. The skill can be taught earlier but you should not expect high levels of inhibition in the young child. Nor is there any need to drug them to calm down; instead, you can teach them the skills of avoiding distractions, which can be done by being careful about the demands we placed on the child.

The second is the ability to shift between different tasks or across ideas. Some refer to this as multitasking, but this is not the best interpretation as we indeed can rarely do two tasks at once. A great way to see this is to watch the Monkey Illusion (www.youtube.com/watch?v=IGQmdoK_ZfY). This shows how you can be so involved in a task that you do not see critical information coming from a different perspective. It is also why being clear with instructions is so critical, because when you give multiple instructions, your child may hear or focus on part of them and not necessarily on the critical part of the task.

The third component is monitoring and updating incoming information, or building the skills to organize and manipulate the contents in the working memory. This involves checking whether the information is still relevant for the task and revising or updating one's thoughts with more relevant information.

Children with problems with any of these three skills often have difficulties in reading and many other school subjects. Helping your pre-school child develop these three skills can make major differences, and there are many ways you can do this. For example, make observations such as can your children appropriately stop their behavior when asked, can they move freely from one situation or activity to another, and can they hold information in their mind for completing a task. Work with them to plan and organize before starting a task, and then pause and evaluate how they are going during the task. Break instructions up step by step and reward them when they memorize instructions and information. Teach them to identify, welcome, and correct errors or missteps during the task, not by telling or scolding them but by helping them to become a learning detective of ways to improve. Pause during reading or doing tasks to shift attention to other tasks and information and then come back to the original task. Invite them to think of other ways to solve problems, and be explicit about the task and the best learning strategies to use. And all the time, be a role model showing what you do when you forget, misinterpret, and self-question and how you respond with flexibility.

There are many, mainly commercial, programs on the web to assist in developing these working memory skills. The evidence shows that while these programs can be some help, the transfer to specific skills (like reading or reducing misbehavior) is weak — indeed, close to zero. Some programs also recommend exercise, mindfulness, and video games, and while these can help, and can be worthwhile in themselves, it is the specific teaching of the skills in the context of real tasks that helps the most.

Let's return to the three components of executive functioning we encountered in Mind frame 4. These are important for the development of your children's self-regulation:[3]

Inhibition is the ability to deliberately inhibit dominant, automatic, or common responses when necessary. A common task to assess inhibition is to show a set of nine color words (e.g., blue, green, yellow) but have each word represented NOT in the color of the word but in a different color (e.g., blue is presented in red). Then ask that you read the words as fast as you can and repeat but call out the colors of the words. The second is harder than the first, because you have to focus on one aspect (the color or the word) while inhibiting the secondary information. The ability to not be distracted by the more obvious features is called inhibition — and we need this skill to avoid the many distractions all around us as we grow and learn. Children diagnosed with ADHD and related behaviors often have low levels of this skill to inhibit. Here's the good news, we can teach inhibition.

Shifting, also termed cognitive flexibility or task switching, is the ability to move back and forth between multiple different tasks. Typically, it is associated with the ability to perform two or more simple decision tasks and to switch between them upon a specific cue or in a specific order. For example, we could ask you to sort a set of cards on color, partway through ask you to sort on the number, and then shift again to having you sort into the picture and non-picture cards. The shifting requires you to process a change of rules, and errors can occur when you are not able to suppress or inhibit the previous set of rules but continue to apply them. There is little evidence to support the notion of multitasking, however. Rather, 'shifting' is the speed of switching our attention from one task to another.

Monitoring and Updating relate to the ability to manipulate the contents being held by working memory. We are humans of little brains in one way, in that there is a limited number of items of information that can be held at any one time, irrespective of ability. Most adults can hold up to three or four items of information in their working memory at any one time. Take 10 seconds to recall these digits:

8   2   6   5   9   7   1   0   6

Now cover up these numbers, get up, and walk to the other end of the room, sing 'Happy Birthday' to yourself. Next, recall the numbers in the order they were presented. Most people recall 3–4 items in the right order. This is not a good or bad thing; it is simply that our brains are constrained to hold limited amounts of stuff in short-term memory. (Some of you might see this as a phone number: 826 597 106, and this means you only have to recall three chunks of information: Chunking is one of the skills you can use to teach your child how to hold more in their working memory.)

All three aspects of executive functioning are particularly important in cognitive development, and they are often a more accurate predictor of the variability of academic achievement than intelligence and IQ. Each component can improve throughout the school years, up to about the age of 16. They then gradually decrease until the early 30s, by which time we have usually worked out how and when to use these three skills to maintain our thinking lives.

You need to be clear about what you mean and what you are asking of your children, but critically you need to ensure that the child heard, understood, and can action what you are asking. This ensures you can help them inhibit the unnecessary parts of any request, focus on what you really mean, and bring it into their immediate working memory. If there are multiple aspects of what you are asking, then you need to be sure they see and understand these shifts and multiple requests.

A powerful way to help children develop the three components of executive functioning (skills of inhibition, shifting, monitoring and updating) is to think and talk to your children in terms of what success looks like. Provide an example of what success looks like and model it, because showing your child the standards of any task (i.e., when 'good is good enough') can help focus their minds on the request and increase the chances of their success.

This progressive development of executive functioning has been linked to the development of the brain. Note, the brain is not a muscle, it is not a machine, but it is a 'wiring and firing' mechanism – it fires neurons and it makes chemical reactions. To use the jargon, we need to create new paths between synapses, or connections between neurons in the central nervous system. The brain is changeable, hence the notion of the plasticity of the brain. But it is not until the major growth spurt in the prefrontal cortex (the front part of the brain), usually between 9–13 years, that your child really starts to have more control over these three components of executive functioning.

Let's look at how the three components of executive functioning – inhibition, shifting, and monitoring and updating – develop with age.[4]

Birth–2 years of age. This is the stage when the brain is forming its largest number of new connections between neurons and the brain increases in size. Between 7–12 months of age there are dramatic increases in the formation of synapses between neurons in the brain. This is also the stage where the child starts to develop an understanding that objects continue to exist even when they cannot be observed, and the child begins to separate thoughts from actions.

From *birth–2 years of age,* frontal areas of the brain, including the prefrontal cortex, increase in area quickly. With these developments, young children begin to attend, learn not to be distracted, hold more ideas in their heads at once, and increase their working memory. The differences in attention during these early childhood years can predict the ability to inhibit responses later in childhood.

2–7 years of age. The critical time for all three aspects of executive functioning is from 3–5 years of age. Inhibition develops at a marginally earlier age than shifting and monitoring and updating. The vast majority of studies suggest that inhibition develops from about 2–5 years of age, with the child inhibiting for increasing periods. For example, the study by Stephanie Carlson[5] saw a dramatic shift in the ability of children to suppress eating treats between the ages of 2–3. In this study, 50% of 2-year-olds were able to hold off eating a treat for 20 seconds. However, 3-year-olds were able to fight the urge for 1 minute. Children younger than 4 years of age find inhibiting what they say or do very difficult. They can often blurt out their feelings or thoughts without thinking or even lash out physically, and such disinhibition shows the child's lack of control over their immediate impulses to do or say something.

There can be rapid developments in the ability to shift between multiple ideas between 2–7 years of age, particularly when you assist the child. There can be dramatic observable changes in updating from 15 months of age until 30 months, large changes in updating ability occurring between the ages of 3–5 years, and a tailing off towards the age of 7. As the child grows, shifting, inhibition and updating tasks that were too complex for children under the ages of 5 subsequently become manageable for children after the age of 5.

7–11 years of age. During these years, the child's thinking becomes more flexible as they can simultaneously combine perspectives, breaking them down into different approaches and ordering them. This steady and maintained growth in executive functioning matches the simultaneous anatomical changes of the prefrontal cortex, the home of planning and attention control. Both inhibition and shifting abilities appear to improve along a linear trajectory, reaching close to adult levels at about 11 years of age. Updating ability, however, continues to improve into adolescence, reaching maturity at about 15 years of age.

11–16 years of age into adulthood. The final stage of Piagetian development, the Formal Operation stage from 11–16 years, is characterized by abstract and hypothetical thought. During this stage, children develop more control over which learning strategies to use, are more able to reflect on their learning, and are more able to consider different perspectives and alternatives.

It is important to appreciate that these skills in thinking develop and change during the 0–15-year age period. Asking students to be attentive, not be distracted, and to consider shifting between multiple requests or ideas may be not possible if the students have not been taught these skills at the right moments during these years. Too often we rush to label those who cannot be attentive, shift between ideas, or update and monitor their thinking. This can condemn them to live with the labels, whereas instead we should be more specific about teaching these skills. Instead of expecting so much from younger children, we should be patient and wait – the skills will develop over time as the brain grows. Do not rush to judgment too quickly, and resist using labels that can set false and low expectations. Once again, Goldilocks comes to the fore – there is a balancing act about labeling – useful for making next steps, not useful for raising expectations.

Labeling can be a major negative. Take two children of the same personality, same levels of inattention, same skills at shifting between ideas, and label one (e.g., disruptive, dyslexic, Asperger's) and not the other. The result is a massive negative impact on the labeled compared to the non-labeled student.[6] We are not saying that autism, Asperger's, and related labels are not real (they are); rather, what we are saying is beware of labels. They are children first, and any label should only mean they may need more intensive interventions to build specific skills. Think of a parallel – when doctors diagnose your ailment, they don't say you are now identified by the label and you are a bad or lesser person; they use the label to implement a treatment. Similarly in schools, labels and diagnoses are but the first steps to teaching programs, and we should not attach the child to a label that condemns them to low and often false expectations.

Back to self-regulation: The ages at which skills of inhibition, shifting, and updating reach adult levels are as follows:

Inhibition reaches adult levels about 11–12 years of age

Shifting does not reach adult levels until about 15 years of age

Updating does not reach adult levels until about 15 years of age

This does not mean the brain stops developing. While you are reading these words on the page there are changes in your brain: The brain is continually renewing, developing synaptic connections, eliminating lowly reinforced synapses. As adults, we are much more able to inhibit distractions, shift between ideas, and update and monitor our thinking, but for our children these are specific skills that need to be taught, and a major constraint on their learning the skills could be the maturation and growth of the brain. You can make a difference by constructing tasks that make it clear which skills are required and what completing the task successfully looks like. You can also be helping your child move between the various components of the task by providing variety rather than requiring a long-term, sustained focus on one aspect.

What is stunning is that this more recent research on brain development and executive functioning is providing support for Piaget's claims made over 70 years ago. We need to remember that the brain changes so much especially between 0–2, but it never stops developing (even at our ages) – and these changes are a function of teaching and learning, not just aging. These changes, and the importance of the early years, highlight why language is so critical in the early years, why we must never give up developing the child's mind and being patient and welcoming and answering their 'why questions', and why it is important to teach your children to inhibit, shift, update, and monitor their thoughts. This teaching is more critical and powerful than drugging them with Ritalin. It is through the development of these three skills that allow your child to make sense of their buzzing, booming, and at times bewildering world.

2 Developing the will – confidence and a growth mindset

Children develop their personality with you, because of you, despite you, and despite you. As parents, you have an enormous influence on this personality development and while a child's skill and thrill are important, you will be known more in terms of the personality of your children than anything else. These personality or disposition aspects relate to what we are 'willing' to do, hence the development of the 'will'. Over the decades, researchers have converged on the Big Five personality attributes (although of course there are squabbles).

The Big Five follow:

- Extraversion – the level of sociability and enthusiasm
- Agreeableness – the level of friendliness and kindness
- Conscientiousness – the level of organization and work ethic
- Emotional stability – the level of calmness and tranquility
- Openness to experiences – the level of creativity and curiosity

All five relate positively but modestly to optimum parenting. One study, for example, looked at the relation of the Big Five to the three major dimensions of the parent–child relationship: warmth, control, and autonomy.[7] Parents scoring high on these three relationship skills may be more able to initiate and maintain positive interactions with their children. In addition, parents who score higher on agreeableness and emotional stability are more supportive of their children's autonomy. However, none of the correlations is high enough to put an over reliance on the personality of the parents.

Similarly, it is hard to claim that a child's personality relates to desirable school outcomes – but to dismiss personality altogether would be to miss the major point. Developing these five factors is worthwhile because it is hard to find evidence that children with lower scores outperform those with higher scores on any socially desired correlate, outcome, or valued attribute in our society. To increase their life chances, you want children to be sociable, friendly, have a work ethic, be calm, and be open to experience.

There is one personality attribute that has a higher relationship with school learning – and that is self-confidence: the confidence to take on challenging tasks, the confidence to seek help, the confidence to work with others to achieve outcomes, the confidence to see themselves as learners, and the confidence to seek and action feedback. The aim is to raise children who are not afraid of being wrong, being challenged, or failing: That is, raise children who dare to be wrong, dare to be challenged, and dare to fail (and learn from this failure). It would not be a challenge if there were no risk of failure. The art is to help your child set challenges according to the Goldilocks principle: not too hard, not too easy, and not too boring.

Watch your child play video games – they set themselves high challenges. This is partly because they know that when they fail they will not be told off or be told they are stupid, partly because they know there are multiple opportunities to practice and learn from playing the game, partly because they are aware of when good is good enough (the notion of success is getting to the next level), and partly because there is no fun playing if the game is too easy. So why not apply these principles in other aspects of their life – school learning, tasks around the house, interacting with siblings, and so on.

Teach your child how to set Goldilocks's criteria of success, give them oodles of options to practice and learn from practice, teach them to monitor their performance relative to the notion of success, and never diss on them when they fail – failure is their best friend as a learner. If instead, you scowl at failure, berate the child if not successful, and do not provide teaching or time to succeed, don't be surprised if your children set safe targets, shy away from challenges, and create safe bubbles in which they work. The result will be a failure to develop the core features of being a successful learner.

One of the current claims is that parents need to teach their students to have grit and to adopt a growth mindset, as this is considered the basis for developing the child's sense of autonomy, competence, and relatedness. Yes, 'grit' and a 'growth mindset' are important. However, these terms are often poorly understood.

Carol Dweck has pioneered the research on growth mindsets and Angela Duckworth has promoted grit as a core notion underlying success.[8] Both have been at pains to note that we all exhibit both growth and fixed mindsets and that grit has a rightful (and wrongful) place (note that criminals and some 'naughty kids' can show high levels of grit). What matters is how children think in times of adversity, failure, and error and when confronted with new and challenging problems and situations: It is in these situations that everyone, children included, needs to display grit (determination) and a growth mindset.

John was asking the highly accomplished and lead teachers at their first Australia national conference who they wanted for the keynote speaker for the next year. The dominant answer was Carol Dweck. Oh, but John knew the effect sizes from growth mindset programs, so how to tell such an eminent researcher that the effects were very low. Panic set in, and a three-course strategy was born over the year before he met Carol and her husband, David, at a fancy restaurant in Sydney.

First course, 'Carol, how do you deal with all the criticism of your work?' It's not fun, but it makes our work better, she said, and you must get it too – so over soup we regaled each other with stories of personal attacks and how the work was misinterpreted and so on.

On to the main course: 'Carol, I don't think there is any such thing as a pure growth mindset'. The knife and fork were lowered, the focused gaze lasered in. 'John, thinking you have a pure growth mindset is often the most fixed mindset of the lot'. Carol noted that she did not believe that people had either growth or fixed mindsets but that we need to teach people the skill of returning to a growth mindset when they fall into a fixed mindset. And even in a growth mindset, you have to know when to give up. 'If I asked you to walk through that wall, I hope you would not do it, rather than saying "I can do it", as you would have a very sore head'.

Without waiting for dessert, John pulled out a large ring binder with every article Carol had written on the subject. 'Carol, I believe there is, but one major occasion when growth versus fixed mindset matters. Listen to what you have said – in times of adversity, challenges, error, failure, helplessness – then having a growth mindset makes a major positive difference. For children struggling to understand or reach the criterion of success, then growth mindsets can make a major difference – but in many tasks where they already have skills, high levels of confidence, and multiple strategies of learning, then a fixed mindset may not be a liability'. We reached agreement, and as Carol explained, she has been at pains to note this over many years. (See www.edweek .org/education/opinion-misinterpreting-the-growth-mindset-why-were-doing-students-a-disservice/2017/06.)

The reason most programs for developing growth, resilience, grit, and mindfulness show small effects is twofold: First, there is an optimal time to use these attributes, and second, most programs aim to teach these attributes in generic programs, but the generalizations fail to transfer to specific situations: We can watch these same students improving their skills on the generic program but then go back to music, physical education, or math and still believe they 'cannot do these subjects'. Indeed, Carol Dweck has described how she killed the first such program (Brainology) because, while it was possible to increase the desired attributes, they failed to transfer to particular situations. She is now working on a more set of programs that are set in various contexts to develop growth thinking. There is an optimal time to use a growth mindset and understanding when to employ it is crucial: When your child fails, is confused, anxious, struggling. Hence, we need to be particularly mindful when your child is in this situation to ensure we see it as an opportunity to learn and improve and not a time to scold because they did not do it right or ignore by praising the effort. Failure needs to be a learner's best friend.

Perhaps if growth and grit are seen as components of high levels of self-confidence to achieve success on tasks, it will help put these two important concepts into the right perspective. If you ask your child to accomplish a task (e.g., 'clean your room'), the core question is whether they have the confidence that they will succeed. So you may need to be more specific about what success looks like before they start (and not measure success in terms of time spent on the task, how much pain and complaining they express, or the opposite – whether they enjoyed the task): Children need to know when they have done a good enough job for it to be considered a success. Then they understand how much 'grit' is needed to successfully complete the task. There are times when a child's grit may stop them learning because sometimes they can be gritty about the wrong stuff; for example, they can hang on to failed strategies and then finally say, 'I cannot do this'. Note that the core notion within good grit is conscientiousness to attend to the task, to seek help, and to learn to monitor progress towards success. Therefore, make the notion of success as transparent as possible, give feedback about the progress toward this success, be available when your child seeks or needs help, and help them persist on the task – in that order and not the reverse.

When children lack the confidence to achieve success, they can often adopt fixed mindsets and blame others, claim they do not have the skills, and avoid engagement. Set smaller steps to lead to success, think about the skills needed for small wins and teach these skills, and value progression toward success – this will reduce anxiety and increase confidence, helping them develop a growth mindset so they can overcome their prior belief that they could not do the task.

Remember, developing these skills is best undertaken with tasks your children feel most uncomfortable with and where there is a high sense of challenge and risk of failure. The development of these skills can occur early in the child's learning. Carol Dweck and colleagues[9] showed that children who chose, or were allowed by their parents, to stop trying to complete a difficult puzzle were more likely to believe that they were incapable of finishing the task and had lower expectations for future performance than those children who chose to persist or were assisted to persist.

If parents then criticized the work of the non-completers, these children lowered their originally positive evaluations of their work and were less likely to say they would do that type of work again less likely to come up with constructive solutions for improving their criticized products. Younger children see their work as 'bad', and as they get older they see this as their lack of ability to learn the skills needed to complete the tasks. Developing confidence, growth mindsets, and grit to achieve worthwhile tasks starts early and is very much influenced by the parents' reactions to failure.

Jessica Lahey wrote a book on the 'gift of failure' and noted how hard it was for her to stop equating the act of doing things for her children with good parenting but instead that good parenting was leaving them to do the things they could do for themselves.[10] She discusses how parents' fear of failure undermines schoolwork and how, for children to become masterpieces, their flaws must be allowed to remain and serve as an essential part of their tale.

Make failure the best friend of learning. Put this poster from Michael Jordan on your wall or one citing Serena Williams: '*A champion isn't about how much they win, it's about how they recover from their downs, whether it's an injury or whether it's a loss*'.

Michael Jordan's concept of learning from errors:

I've missed more than 9000 shots in my career. I've lost almost 300 games. 26 times, I've been trusted to take the game-winning shot and missed. I've failed over and over and over again in my life. And that is why I succeed.

This is a major reason to be wary about praising the 'child' while AT THE SAME TIME providing feedback or comments on their work or activities. They recall the part that is about them – the praise – and overlook the feedback on their work. Give lots of praise, yes, but separate it from feedback about the task. Do not dilute feedback about a task with praise about the person doing the task. Too often the praise reinforces the notion that it is something within the child that caused the lack of learning, whereas we want our children to realize that while they may not yet be reaching a particular level, with openness to teaching they CAN learn and complete tasks to higher levels of performance.

Bottom line: In times of not knowing, struggle, and errors children need to be taught that these are opportunities to learn, and NOT statements about their limits, capabilities, or lack of skill to learn. As we've said before, failure must become a learner's best friend. Parents who only seek to correct or who expect perfect performances are failing their children. Parents who do not themselves learn in the face of adversity provide poor role models. Learn to fail and enjoy learning from the failure with your children. That is how you develop the mindset that it can be done, it is worth investing in trying harder tasks, it is worth taking on more difficult challenges, and it is worth focusing on learning, learning, learning.

3 Developing the thrill – passion and investment

How do you motivate your child to become a great learner? When you ask a child why they've done something, this presumes the child intentionally set out to do whatever it was they did – but not everything people do is caused by an intention, a thought, or a motive. Children rarely sit still – they propel, they act, they move – this way or that – and not everything is premeditated, thought through, or considered (it's the same for adults). Motivation relates to *choosing* to engage, act, or invest in actions. Often when a parent asks a child why they've done something, the parent is seeking more than an explanation – often they are asking the child for a justification of why they did this rather than that or rather than not doing it at all. Such questioning about motives can be emotionally charged and is not the best approach.

A better approach is to talk to children about their motivation to do a task in terms of their notion of what success means, their expectations about how they intend to get to the goal or success, what they will do if things do not go smoothly on the journey to the goal, how confident they are that they will be successful, and the likely implications (emotionally and achievement-wise) if they do or do not achieve their goal.

Children can be motivated by wanting to master the task; want to look good in front of friends, siblings, or you; for some intrinsic or extrinsic reward; or for the reason some people climb Mount Everest – because it is there. Motivation can be because the task is worthwhile and fun to do, because it is part of future planning and seen to be useful, or because there is value in the act of doing the task.

Motivation can also come from wanting to prevent outcomes, such as looking bad or not succeeding, or to avoid loss and embarrassment. Success or failure can be attributed to oneself or to other factors (she made me do it, it wasn't my fault, it got in the way, it was bad luck). People are more likely to attribute success to their efforts and failure to someone or something else. Such confirmation bias is very common (and everyone does it).

What about rewards for good work, good behavior, and success? We have already discussed one of the most powerful and supported theories of motivation – the self-determination model. This model is based on the premise that all human beings have the fundamental needs to feel related, competent, and autonomous in order to develop and function optimally. These three needs can be enhanced particularly when your child plays an active role in their own development.

You can develop these attributes by being clear about limits such as providing rationales and explanations about the task up front and when your children request help. You also need to recognize the feelings and perspective of the child, offer choices, encourage initiative, and be aware of the child's emotions (particularly any sense of guilt, worry, anxiety, lack of confidence). Also, it is important to minimize the use of controlling techniques – which is not to be confused with permissiveness, a lack of structure, or neglect. Indeed, a lack of structure and a sense of chaos in the home are negative and to be avoided. Krysta Andrews and colleagues found a negative relation to the development of executive functioning in homes where there is frenetic activity, a lack of structure, unpredictability in everyday activities, and high levels of ambient stimulation (e.g., noise and clutter).[11]

Success requires a gradual release of responsibility by the parent to allow the child to complete the task. The parent should also, during and after completion, attribute the success or failure to the child's actions. Parents are responsible for ensuring the child knows, upfront, what the task involves, and what successful completion looks like. Parents also provide the structures to maximize success, and they listen to how the child has thought about their actions and the task.

An oft-asked question is whether children are more motivated when there is an external reward. The answer has been clear for many decades: NO, do not resort to rewards and bribery. If a reward is unexpected and not based on mere participation or doing the task, it is not so bad. But when a reward is the reason for doing the task, the longer term effects are not good at all. This is particularly so when the reward is administered in a controlling fashion by the parent because this diminishes the child's development of their own sense of control over the task and any personal incentive to continue to do the task.

Ed Deci and colleagues completed a synthesis of 128 studies that show the presence of rewards systematically undermines intrinsic motivation ($d = -0.24$).[12] The largest negatives were from tangible rewards ($d = -0.34$), completion rewards ($d = -0.44$), participation rewards ($d = -0.28$), and gold star – type rewards such as money, material goods, and prizes ($d = -0.34$). Positive effects on outcomes were more related to verbal rewards IF the task was completed in a low controlling manner by the parent (or teacher). When the extrinsic reward was unexpected, the effect was not negative but was zero. So, it does not matter if you want to unexpectedly reward (verbal or tangible), but it does not help either.

This finding about the low to negative effect of rewards often surprises many as we all seem to like rewards, stickers, and praise – but the point is that this does not convert into deeper engagement in learning. Instead, we become motivated to seek the reward, and when we do not get it, we lose interest in the task that led to the reward. The message is to not be concerned with rewards for motivating children's actions and behaviors but facilitate more interesting tasks, more choice within these tasks, to ensure they are appropriately challenging, provide structures of support with a gradual release of responsibility to the child, and set up trusting environments where failure is seen as an opportunity to learn and seek help. We want children to learn to master and not merely complete tasks because of factors external to the joy, value, and positive learning from the task. Remember they play their video games to move to the next level – the reward is more challenge and more learning.

The message is: Do not be concerned with rewards for motivating children's actions and behaviors. Rather, facilitate more interesting tasks and provide more choice within these tasks to ensure they are appropriately challenging, provide support with a gradual release of responsibility to the child, and set up trusting environments where failure is seen as an opportunity to learn and seek help. You want children to learn to master a task, not merely to complete a task because of factors external to the joy, value, and positive learning from the task. Remember, children play their video games to move to the next level – the reward is more challenge and more learning.

Concluding comments

In every learning situation, your child brings their skills, will, and sense of thrill and these are also the three attributes we wish to enhance – separately or collectively. Our expectations must not be that these are set and unchangeable but that they can be enhanced as, more than anything else, your expectations are visible to your child.

Notes

1 Sulloway, F. J. (1995). Birth order and evolutionary psychology: A meta-analytic overview. *Psychological Inquiry, 6*(1), 75–80.
2 Miller, G. A. (1956). The magical number seven, plus or minus two: Some limits on our capacity for processing information. *Psychological Review, 63*(2), 81.
3 Miyake, A., Friedman, N. P., Emerson, M. J., Witzki, A. H., Howerter, A., & Wager, T. D. (2000). The unity and diversity of executive functions and their contributions to complex "frontal lobe" tasks: A latent variable analysis. *Cognitive Psychology, 41*(1), 49–100.
4 Bolton, S., & Hattie, J. (2017). Cognitive and brain development: Executive function, Piaget, and the prefrontal cortex. *Archives of Psychology, 1*(3).
5 Carlson, S. M. (2005). Developmentally sensitive measures of executive function in preschool children. *Developmental Neuropsychology, 28*(2), 595–616.
6 Fuchs, D., Fuchs, L. S., Mathes, P. G., Lipsey, M. W., & Roberts, P. (2002). Is "learning disabilities" just a fancy term for low achievement? A meta-analysis of reading differences between low achiever with and without the label. In R. Bradley, L. Danielson, & D. P. Hallahan (Eds.), *Identification of learning disabilities: Research to practice. The LEA series on special education and disability* (pp. 737–762). Lawrence Erlbaum Associates.

7 Prinzie, P., Stams, G. J. J., Deković, M., Reijntjes, A. H., & Belsky, J. (2009). The relations between parents' Big Five personality factors and parenting: A meta-analytic review. *Journal of Personality and Social Psychology*, *97*(2), 351.

8 Dweck, C. (2017). *Mindset-updated edition: Changing the way you think to fulfil your potential*. Hachette. Duckworth, A. (2016). *Grit: The power of passion and perseverance* (Vol. 234). Scribner.

9 Burhans, K. K., & Dweck, C. S. (1995). Helplessness in early childhood: The role of contingent worth. *Child Development*, *66*(6), 1719–1738.

10 Lahey, J. (2015). *The gift of failure*. HarperCollins.

11 Andrews, K. (2020). *Household chaos, maternal distress and parenting: Associations with child function across multiple domains*. Unpublished doctoral dissertation, McMaster University.

12 Deci, E. L., Koestner, R., & Ryan, R. M. (1999). A meta-analytic review of experiments examining the effects of extrinsic rewards on intrinsic motivation. *Psychological Bulletin*, *125*(6), 627.

5

I love learning

1 *The brain is developing from conception to cremation*

- The brain continues to change, especially as it moves from sensorimotor operations to preoperational (thinking symbolically) to concrete operational to formal operational (thinking abstractly).

- Learning is driven by what we refer to as executive functioning, which relates to *how we manage and think about thinking, doing, caring, emoting, relating, acting and much more.*

- There are three major components to executive functioning: the ability to concentrate and not be distracted or act impulsively, the ability to shift between different tasks or across ideas, and the art of monitoring and updating incoming information for task relevance.

2 *The role of play in learning*

- In the early years it is less play, play, play but more language, language, language – which can be developed during play.

3 *What is learning? – the message from computer games*

- We can learn much about learning from computer gaming: the power and thrill of challenge, failure, error detection, feedback, curiosity, narrative, emotion, pacing, the many roles of the learner, and playing the game of learning is the reward.

This chapter aims to foster your child's love of learning. It outlines the three critical processing tasks that need attention, particularly in the early years and then again during adolescence: the ability to concentrate and not be distracted, the ability to shift across tasks, and the art of monitoring and updating information.

     DOI: 10.4324/9781003257028-7

When I (KH) was a child, I was not, or at least I didn't think I was, a good learner. I took a long time to get concepts, when things got hard I would doubt myself, and I did the bare minimum to get by. This was the same in primary, in secondary, and even in university. I found learning hard, and I did not have a positive attitude toward learning. I stuck at it because I knew what I wanted to do in life; funnily enough, that was to go back to school as a teacher.

When I started to work as a teacher at a newly opened school, I was responsible for developing a learning model for all classes. It was then that I started to understand what learning actually looks like. I thought, 'Wow, if only I had known this when I was younger'. After a few years of teaching with a learning model and teaching learners how to use it, I went back to university.

This time I needed to put more emphasis on how well I did because I needed a B+ average for the whole course. I instantly thought back to my earlier university way of thinking, which was just do what you need to pass – 'Cs get degrees'. I tried my new ways of learning, with an emphasis on seeing 'not knowing' as an opportunity to seek feedback, to talk with peers about what I did and did not understand, and to see the difference between knowing lots and relating the ideas. When I finished my first paper, I finished with a B+. I had done it. This brought my confidence up a lot, and I wanted to prove that it was not a fluke. Next paper same result, an A– and so on, A, and then A+. I had finished my whole postgraduate diploma with an A, average. This was never something that I had experienced before. I could not believe it. I had finally figured out how to learn. It was all about seeing 'not knowing' as a positive, and it really worked.

There used to be much debate as to what matters most in learning and development: what you are born with or the environment. The former was based on the claim that once born, a person's potentials were set; the latter is summed up by the Jesuit claim 'give me a child for the first seven years and I will give you the adult'. However, neither of these extreme claims is correct, as the brain is changing all the time because of its interaction with the environment, even as you read this paragraph. Appreciating these changes in the brain means that we can become increasingly aware of the pivotal role we play in the development of a child's thinking and learning. This chapter outlines these major brain changes.

1 The brain is developing from conception to cremation

We have already met Jean Piaget. As a youngster, he was fascinated with natural history. In his early teens he wrote a paper on mollusks, went on to finish his PhD, and then worked with Alfred Binet and Théodore Simon – the original developers of the first intelligence tests. Piaget became more interested in the errors that children made when completing the tests and studied (among many others) his own three children and how they explained their (wrong) answers. The study of 'error' has a long history, and we will return to it in the next mind frame. His observations about his children led him to develop the four-stage model of mental development that still has much value today for understanding how your child's thinking develops.

Recall from earlier the study where he showed children how to pour a beaker of water into a wide squat glass and into a narrow tall glass. The amount of water did not change, but children up to about 4–5 years would swear the tall glass had more water. Only after their brains develop to a certain point could they appreciate that it was the same amount of water. He conducted many of these studies showing how children reasoned differently, and he proposed four major stages that children grow through. Of course, he had his critics, and today he is mostly taught in child development as a historical figure. For our purposes, however, we introduce some of Piaget's findings to help you see as a parent the different world views that your child can have and to learn to stand in their shoes to understand their reasoning.

Recall that Piaget's four stages relate to how the child thinks and reasons differently as they grow.

JEAN PIAGET'S FOUR STAGES

The Sensorimotor Stage – Birth–2 years. The child experiences their world through movement, and they begin to learn that things continue to exist even if they cannot be seen (e.g., peekaboo), that people and things are different, and that their actions can cause things to happen in the world around them. It is through manipulating objects and being engaged in experiences where the most learning occurs. This is the time to focus on talking, talking, talking as the child will be listening and absorbing information. It is the time to provide sensory experiences of new environments, to expand their skills, help them differentiate between objects, and allow them to experience the multiple ways of the world around them.

The Preoperational Stage: 2–7 years. During this stage, children begin to think symbolically and learn to use words and pictures to represent objects. This is where your early focus on talking and language really pays off, as they build ideas and words about interpreting the world around them, and begin to see the world from the perspective of others. By pretend play, they can develop thinking about the world and about others around them, but they are still quite concrete (what you see is what you get) – such as claiming the taller-than-wider glass has more water or that a rolled ball of clay is more than a flattened piece, even though they can see they started the same size.

The Concrete Operational Stage: 7–11 years. Your child improves their skills in thinking logically about concrete events, comes to understand that the two glasses of water hold the same amount, and begins to use reasoning from specific to forming general principles. Their egocentrism starts to be reduced, and here is where they explore how others might view a situation. They can still struggle with abstract and hypothetical concepts.

The Formal Operational Stage: 12-plus years. The ability to think abstractly and reason about hypothetical problems is the major feature of this stage. They can engage in more abstract thought, think about moral and social issues, begin to use deductive logic reasoning from a general principle to specific information, and think more abstractly.

Since Piaget's work, other researchers have shown that the progression is not this simple; children can be across more than one stage, and there can be cultural differences. Some theorists have added substages and other details to Piaget's model, but the four stages remain a useful conceptual framework for understanding how a child's thinking develops.

About 40–60% of adults never reach or stay in the formal operational stage, and children, as they grow older, can revert to previous stages. For example, ask many adults about astronomy, politics, and biology and you will often hear concrete operational thinking. Entry into higher stages can be speeded up by appropriate schooling.

Trying to reason with a child mainly operating in the concrete stage is almost futile, and not encouraging a child in the concrete operational stage to think aloud about consequences and 'what ifs' is a missed opportunity. It is convenient (and adults still do it) to say, 'I did not know', 'I didn't see it', 'How could I have predicted that', and revert to the lower stages to avoid criticism and responsibility. Your role as parent is to first recognize the nature of thinking and reasoning your child is doing now and advance them gently, gently into the next level of thinking: gentle persuasion, relentlessly pursued.

Piaget would have been excited to have today's modern technology to see inside the brain and follow the massive changes in the brain as a child grows. The brain at birth is but the starting base for later growth. The environment can dramatically shape the building, the realization of full potential, and the way we use the brain we have been given.

2 The role of play in learning

There is everything right about play, but play can be overrated. One of the core beliefs in our society relates to the value of play. When you finish reading this section, your faith in play will be maintained but you may question some of the overblown claims, especially when it comes to developing the core learning skills we are talking about in this book.

Play has major benefits for social and emotional development and learning turn taking and social etiquette, but it has a poor record for learning about learning. Antoine Lillard and colleagues[1] completed a major review of pretend play and struggled to find evidence to support the claim that play helps develop problem-solving. They found it may have a small role in developing executive functioning and social skills but certainly does not drive development. Wow, this shook us to the core. They showed how children choose the level of play relative to their intelligence and they do not become more intelligent from then engaging in this play. What is needed is increased challenge.

A common claim is that play is crucial to development. It allows the child to explore their environment, create fantasy worlds, separate actions from reality, be an indicator of development, and much more. But if play is this important, should we not then expect to see a correlation with learning attributes we value, such as developing a theory of mind (i.e., way of viewing the world), increased use of language, and greater achievement on tasks?

There is no convincing evidence that play develops children's 'theory of mind', and there is little support that pretend play improves or is even crucial to the development of self-regulation. Lillard and colleagues concluded: 'The literature reviewed here does not support the view that pretend play is crucial for children's cognitive development' (p. 13).

But there is an alternative: Involve the child in more 'playful learning'. Compared with free-play programs, more structured classrooms with carefully designed, challenging, hands-on activities that confer learning appear to help children's development the most. It does not matter who initiates the learning – what matters is the number and challenge of learning opportunities. Just as important is the amount and range of language in the play. John Church from the University of Canterbury often said that if choosing between a play center or keeping the child in your home, listen to where there is most language and place your child there. It is the same with play: It can be a powerful way to teach the language of learning, that is, to help your child learn about learning, to learn various strategies of learning, to know what to do when they do not know what to do (e.g., seek help), and to monitor their progress to success in the activity.

3 What is learning? – the message from computer games

Kyle went through a phase of excessive time playing video games (so did his dad). We know many parents who worry about their children coming home, going straight to their room and playing. We heard of the many debates about video games and kids nowadays becoming addicted to video games. But think about what video games do for kids. As a parent you would love for your child to follow instructions, work toward something, actively listen, pay more attention, communicate more, solve problems, be okay with trying new things, be determined, and be more resilient. When playing video games, kids do all these things. So what is it about video games that bring all these qualities that you and your child's teachers are trying to encourage out of kids? Video games are designed to get progressively harder as the game progresses; they know the skills of how to turn kids on to learning. We have much to learn from them.

Our children have grown up in the era of computer games, and many of us as adults have indulged in playing these games. John became a master at Space Invaders, graduated to Game Boys, and later to Angry Birds. John introduced Kyle to sudoku, and we played most days together until Kyle systematically could beat his dad (Kyle could recall all the unused numbers in his head, and John had to write them down, which took precious extra minutes). We know many kids today spend eons of time playing Fortnight, and many other online games. The media often screams about the adverse effects and blames societal evils on, war games, and many have proclaimed the end of civilization from such games.

So why do games have such a fascination and what can we learn from them about what it means to learn? Here are 15 things to learn and apply as parents.

1 MAKE SURE THE INVOLVEMENT IN THE TASK IS EQUALLY AS REWARDING, IF NOT MORE SO THAN THE GOAL

Most video games have a goal, with many steps in the process of getting to the goal – however, the aim is not necessarily to reach the goal but to learn to master the many steps in this process. I recall playing Mario Bros on the Gameboy and one eventful afternoon I had a major problem. I got to the end! I did not want the game to end – I wanted to keep playing. The aim is the game of learning, the game of meeting challenging success levels, the game of mastering the game. But often, instead of allowing our children to enjoy the challenges, we tell them to aim for the goal and get there as fast as possible. If time is up before the goal is reach, we lower the criteria of success by saying, 'You did you best', 'Well done', or if they reach the goal (complete the task), we reward them by saying now they can go and play. Instead, we need to invest them in the fun of learning and the rewards of meeting a series of challenges. The art is in making transparent up front what the next criterion of success looks like, providing multiple opportunities to deliberately practice, and making the learning as critical and enjoyable as reaching the goal. The reward can be mastery and does not need to be an external reward.

2 THE THRILL IS IN THE CHALLENGE – NOT TOO HARD, NOT TOO EASY, NOT TOO BORING

Children play games, not because they are easy but because they are hard. The gaming industry has worked out the Goldilocks principle of challenge – not too hard, not too easy, and not too boring. The games hit the sweet spot between anxiety and boredom. Such 'flow', as it is often called, means that learning is 'just above' the level of performance and what a person could achieve with lots of practice, and with just-in-time feedback and help from an expert (often in games, a peer who has mastered that level). Give your child tasks according to the Goldilocks principle, make the criteria of success (in games, the next level) very clear, and provide the learning to help them attain the goal and enjoy the process of learning.

3 LEARNERS LOVE FAILURE

When playing video games, you have multiple opportunities to fail, and that is more than okay – it provides the opportunity to learn. There is no fear of failure because failure is part of the enjoyment – no failure would mean the game is too easy and therefore no fun. Beware of becoming the Tiger Mom who drives the fun out of learning – the child is doing the tasks for fear of rebuke because they have to. It is no wonder many of these children drift away from investing in learning when the tiger loses its influence and claws. There must be intrinsic motivation to learn, a safe environment to learn from failing often, and an awareness that mistakes are not bad but necessary to reach a solution.

4 HELP IDENTIFY ENABLERS AND BARRIERS

Every challenging task and problem will have enablers and barriers – otherwise, it would not be a challenge. In many cases, the first step is helping the child build the skills to recognize these barriers (knowing the problem is halfway to the solution). Helping them become problem-solvers is the essence of developing learners. In one school where Kyle taught, each week each child was given a situation and had to work out the problem (not the answer). For example, in the week John visited, a Year 3 student had a locker and had to work out where it was broken and possible reasons for the break. In many games, there can be opportunities to learn new information, models, exemplars, resources, and tools that can facilitate problem-solving – this is also your role as a parent.

5 MAXIMIZE FEEDBACK

Feedback needs to be just-in-time, just-for-me, and focused on 'where to next'. Yes, feedback about current performance, about *how* you are progressing is valuable, but unless it is also accompanied with feedback about where to go next it is often not seen as worthwhile. Imagine sitting down with your spouse and saying, 'We are going to have a feedback session. Now here is what you are doing wrong, here is where you are not meeting your goals, here is how you are not progressing'. Ouch. But maybe 'How can we work together to decide where we go next in raising our kids', might work. The mistake we often make with feedback is believing that feedback given is feedback understood. Nope, the key is to work out whether your child heard the feedback, understood the feedback, and is able to action the feedback. That is what video games aim for – give feedback in context, give it as often as needed to be understood, and make sure the feedback is aimed at improvement and answering the 'where to next' question.

6 BE CURIOUS AND CURIOUSER

There is a freedom to experiment, explore, and see 'what if'. You can explore the consequences of your actions (and not wait for the 'you are naughty', 'that is wrong', 'bad person). The pleasure is in the discovery.

7 WHO'S IN CONTROL?

Most games give a sense of control to the user. Imagine playing a game that takes back control, plays the game itself, and then gives the boring parts of the player. They would not work. But often this is how kids see you when you ask them to do something. They get the boring bits, the leftovers, the tasks you do not enjoy doing. How can you give them some control over decisions that lead to enjoyable learning, engagement in the task, and decisions of the best ways to achieve the task?

8 YOU LEARN TO PLAY THE GAME IN THE MIDST OF PLAYING THE GAME

Assigning a task to your child and then leaving them to it presumes they have the skills, they know what success looks like, and they will not make a mistake. Ensure there are (safe) learning opportunities while doing the task, that there are no adverse consequences if they seek help or do not succeed at first and increase the chances that they can learn and improve while doing the task.

9 MAKE SURE THERE IS A STORY IN WHICH PROBLEMS ARE EMBEDDED. WE READ FOR THE NARRATIVE, NOT FOR THE PHONICS

Games involve a narrative – it is not doing for the sake of doing, but there is a story such that you want to be immersed in the story, hear more about the story, and quest for an active role affecting the story's direction and outcomes. Learning is through participating in the story. During the story, there can be many opportunities for reflection, evaluation, illustration, exemplification, and inquiry. How much of a compelling narrative is there in the tasks you ask of your child? In many games, children are placed in scenarios where they must understand and synthesize diverse information and analyze and work out strategies. The narrative helps provide a context and motivation and fire the emotions. There are plot hooks that keep the player guessing, uncertainties that encourage problem-solving and exploration, twists that create intrigue and frame puzzles, clues and information embedded in the task, and fun in playing. Nearer the end of the story the many parts are built into a reveal, often unanticipated, but all the time the reward is in the playing.

10 LEARNING CAN BE EMOTIONAL

Listen to your kids playing video games – you hear the learning, you hear the emotions, you hear the angst, failure, and success aloud. Do you hear these emotions when you ask your kid to do a task? We need to invoke the emotions of learning. Game designers allow the player to feel toward the character in the game; they are often specific about the emotions about to be experienced and involve characters with strengths and weaknesses but who are allowed to grow and improve during the game.

11 LEARNING IS BEST TIED TO PAST PERFORMANCE

We spend a lot of time telling our kids they will need this in their future, you will be grateful for this one day, it will get you a job later. This is just not believable as, more often than not, it is just not true. Much more powerful is to relate the new task and the learning to what they know already. David Ausubel, a famous educational psychologist, claimed the most important single factor influencing learning is what the learner already knows.[2] Two other researchers added that 'when we learn new material, we do not do so in a vacuum. In fact, we have a very hard time learning new information that is unstructured or random.[3] Computer games are aware of your prior learning – they have your last score and many also keep information about your strategies and times and can alter future experiences based on this information – not to trick you but to make the challenges more appropriate to you.

12 IT'S FUN TO LEARN TOGETHER

Many video games involve others – in person, on screen, via the internet. Kids love the sense of belonging, and enjoy learning and teaching each other. Some like to be competitive and win at all costs, some play to develop mastery, some are wanderers who desire new and fun experiences, and others enjoy the social interaction or involvement in an alternative world. One of the fundamental skills desired by employers is social sensitivity and the skills of working in teams, translating what you know to others in the team, understanding others' points of view (the basis of respect for others), and collaborating to achieve goals. Turn taking is built into many video games, and children learn these rules and have major incentives to learn from others. They also can develop confidence that the group can collectively provide better solutions than any one individual. This is so unlike a lot of schooling where our worth too often is measured by what we achieve alone.

13 WE CAN AMBLE, TROT, GALLOP – WE CAN WORK AT OUR PACE

Videos work like a GPS – we can all have similar success criteria (the same destination), but there can be multiple pathways and variable times to get there. Not everyone has to travel down Highway 1 to get from A to B; some will go off the highway to have less traffic, some to take the scenic route, and some may just get lost on the way. Different routes will take different times to get to the destination. Likewise, video games do not insist all players take the same time to complete the game. The same should apply to learning.

14 THERE ARE MANY ROLES AS A LEARNER

There is rarely one right way, and often traveling the wrong way allows the discovery of better ways, it can be scenically enjoyable to deviate, and there can be multiple roads worth traveling. In video games, the designers allow for these multiple roads and multiple roles while traveling.[4] When problem-solving, it is sometimes worth inviting your child into different roles that can engage them and power them to be better learners. There is the role of the hero, who sees the world through their own eyes; the teacher who provides explanations for the learning and teaches others to play the game; the strategist who reflects, analyzes, plans, and evaluates their and others' moves; the signaler who anticipates moves, using 'what if' ideas, and loves the twists in the plot; the doubter who likes the arguments and uses persuasion to achieve their goals; the shadow who walks beside or slightly behind another and can turn out to be the solver as they learn the skills of watching and reflecting others' moves; and the trickster who offers comic relief and loves additional bumps in the road.

15 WE ARE OF LITTLE MEMORY, AND LEARNING COSTS BRAIN POWER

Computer gamers are aware of cognitive theories about how students learn. There is a great theory developed by John Sweller called cognitive load theory. Game designers have used this theory to capture the imagination, attention, and involvement of our kids – we can learn from this. The model is based on the limited amount we can hold in our short-term working memory at any one time. You may recall from the example earlier that most of us can hold between four to six things in our short-term memory at once. Now imagine we ask you a problem which includes knowing 9 × 6. If you have to pause and work out the answer you are using some of this precious working memory, and it is less likely you have the time or mental capacity to use it in the problem, compared with someone who has over-learned the times tables and isn't relying on their short-term memory capacity.

Help your child manage the load on their short-term memory by making the instructions clear and checking they are understood. Be clear about the problem so the child is not diverted to solving irrelevant problems. Provide worked examples, but take care not to include too much information or pitch the example at too high a level, because this can be demotivating. Ensure the child has sufficient knowledge for the problem at hand so they are not floundering through a lack of knowledge – make sure the important information is the most immediately available, but do not swamp them with detail.

In terms of potential adverse effects from gaming, Christopher Ferguson[5] synthesized 101 studies about the effects of playing video games and found virtually zero effects on increased aggression ($r = .06$), reduced prosocial behavior ($r = .04$), reduced academic performance ($r = -.01$), depressive symptoms ($r = .04$), and attention deficit symptoms ($r = .03$). We need to be wary of thinking about video games as either good or bad, or violent or prosocial, and so having good or bad effects on players. We have a lot to learn about learning from understanding how video games can be so attractive to young people.

Concluding comments

If you show you love learning, it is more likely your child will too. This means thinking aloud about how we go about thinking and solving problems and dilemmas, showing appropriate emotions to learning (emoting about mistakes and successes), how to work with others, and believe that when working with others they can come up with better answers than doing it alone, and teaching the skills of executive functioning: not be distracted, shift between tasks, and monitor and update. We can do this with fun, with passion, and with curiosity. Learning can be playful, but some play may not lead to learning.

Notes

1 Lillard, A. S., Lerner, M. D., Hopkins, E. J., Dore, R. A., Smith, E. D., & Palmquist, C. M. (2013). The impact of pretend play on children's development: A review of the evidence. *Psychological Bulletin, 139*(1), 1.

2 Ausubel, D. P., Novak, J. D., & Hanesian, H. (1968). *Educational psychology: A cognitive view.* Rinehart and Winston.

3 Hattie, J., & Yates, G. C. (2013). *Visible learning and the science of how we learn.* Routledge.

4 Vogler, C. (1998). *The writer's journey: Mythic structures for writers.* Michael Wiese Productions.

5 Ferguson, C. J. (2015). Do angry birds make for angry children? A meta-analysis of video game influences on children's and adolescents' aggression, mental health, prosocial behavior, and academic performance. *Perspectives on Psychological Science, 10*(5), 646–666.

6

I know the power of feedback and success thrives on errors

1 The power of feedback

- *Feedback is powerful but also variable in its effectiveness.*

- *Feedback is important for answering the 'Where to next?' question based on 'Where am I going?' and 'How am I going?'*

- *It is important to vary the nature of feedback depending on whether it relates to a task or content (correct/incorrect, let me show you how), process (let's work together to improve), or self-regulation (you try first to improve).*

- *It is important to appreciate how your feedback is heard, understood, and actioned.*

2 The role of praise

- *Praise given at the same time as feedback usually dilutes the feedback message.*

- *Praise can enhance building a trusting relation.*

- *Feedback can cost more than it is worth.*

3 Learning and feedback feed on errors

- *Feedback is more likely to have a positive impact when there are errors and mistakes than when there is success and correctness.*

- *To make failure a best friend of learning requires relationships of high trust and safety to explore.*

DOI: 10.4324/9781003257028-8

■ *Feedback is effective when it (1) clarifies success, (2) informs the learner of progress relative to success, (3) offers guidance about the next steps to improve, (4) is given and received in a high-trust environment, and (5) when it is heard, understood, and actionable.*

This chapter focuses on a key attribute of successful parenting – the skills of giving and receiving feedback. But while feedback is powerful, it is also variable in its effectiveness. The major factor in ensuring the feedback is heard, understood, and actioned are outlined, and a major message is the critical role of errors and mistakes and how parents need to make failure your child's best friend in developing their learning. Feedback works better when errors are seen as welcomed and expected in their learning.

You will all have received feedback – some of it is wanted, some not, some valuable, some not . . . and therein lies the dilemma of feedback. It can be powerful, but it is variable. Extensive research in schools has found feedback remains one of the more powerful influences on learning, but again it is variable.[1] There is a lot from this school research that applies to the home. For starters, the following commonly held beliefs are in fact myths:

■ We should use the feedback sandwich – give praise followed by corrective feedback, and then more praise. Instead, do not dilute the corrective feedback by adding praise, as your child will recall and focus on the praise. Nothing wrong with praise, just not at the same time as corrective feedback.

■ Feedback should be immediate. If the feedback refers to a task where it can be immediately corrected then maybe, but for a longer lasting impact, often delaying feedback can be more powerful.

■ The more feedback the better; quantity is not the key, ensuring the feedback is heard, understood and actionable is – and sometimes we can reduce the amount of feedback (which is not actioned) to make our feedback more actionable.

1 The power of feedback

Feedback is information provided to reduce the gap between what the child now understands or is doing and what they are aiming to understand. So the first message is (a) *the power of feedback is higher when you have a great understanding of what the child is now doing,*

(b) *when you have a clear understanding of when 'good is good enough'* (that is the desired performance or action), and (c) *your feedback helps your child move from now to the goal.*

Note, nothing in the preceding says anything about praise, about whether the feedback message is positive or negative, or the timing or the tone of the feedback, but rather, the feedback is simply information that moves the child closer to the desired outcome.

Feedback that moves the child's learning on will depend on several factors:

a You must know where the child is now – what is the baseline, what is their current state. The child will feel disappointed and aggrieved if you 'do not understand' their current emotional state, their beliefs about what is occurring. Not knowing where your child is at leads to inappropriate or irrelevant feedback.

b You have a clear idea of what is desired from the feedback, and the child is also clear about the outcome. Feedback is more powerful if the child has understood, up front, what the desired outcome is. This gives them direction, they can interpret the feedback as helping them get to the outcome, and they see some value in achieving the outcome.

c It helps if the child has some commitment to the outcome, although this is not necessary (otherwise, many rooms would never be tidied, and homework never completed).

In our research, we have asked thousands of teachers what they mean by feedback, and the following list captures their answers:

1 Comments – give comments on the way a child is doing something
2 Clarification – answer your child's questions
3 Criticism – give constructive criticism
4 Confirmation – tell your child they are doing it right
5 Content development – provide deeper information
6 Constructive reflection – give your child positive and constructive reflections on their work or performance
7 Correction – show what the child did right or what they did wrong
8 Cons and pros – identifying the pros and cons of their work
9 Criteria – give guidance relative to a standard

All of these nine forms of feedback help the child know 'where they are meant to be aiming' and 'how they are going' toward the goal. What is fascinating is that when you ask children what they mean by feedback, they rarely name these two questions. Instead, they want to know 'Where do I go next?' and 'How do I get there?'

There is nothing wrong with giving the previously mentioned nine forms of feedback, but to make this feedback all the more effective, make sure you also give 'where to next' feedback – that is, *make sure you give feedback that helps the child more forward to the goal.*

From the child's viewpoint, feedback should be such that it propels them to the goal. Consider an obvious example: 'No, that's not right, do it again'. There is no information in this statement to move the child forward, so no wonder it has a low to negative impact. 'No, that's not right, let me show you how to do it' has information to move forward to the goal. It is not the negative or positive; it is the information to feed forward that matters.

You do not want to turn your child into a 'feedback junkie' who becomes so overly dependent on feedback that they continually say, 'What do I do now?' In most situations there are at least three levels for which you can provide feedback: feedback about the task itself, feedback where you work with the child to help them understand how they are doing, and feedback that helps the child monitor their own performance.

- Feedback about the task itself – feedback that identifies whether the task has been done correctly or incorrectly, reshows the child how to do it, and provides more information and direction on how to do it.

- Feedback about how the child is accomplishing the task (the processes) – feedback that is more related to the processes and actions the child uses (or used) to accomplish the task. Such feedback helps the child understand the mistakes they made, can provide different strategies to accomplish the task, and points out relations and connections between what they are doing and how best to move forward.

- Feedback about the child thinking and evaluating their own actions – feedback that helps the child monitor and evaluate their own performance provides confidence in the correctness and direction they are taking and teaches them to ask for feedback rather than waiting for it.

The major message on giving feedback is: Feedback needs to be aimed at either the task, the processes, or letting the child make their own decisions about moving forward. Be clear when giving feedback you choose the optimal form of feedback.

If you say, 'You have made an error, fix it' and they are still learning to do the task and have little understanding of the processes, the feedback is not going to have an impact (other than lead to a negative emotion). If the child has become reasonably accomplished at the task and you say, 'No let me show you how to do it', similarly the effect will be lower as they are at a mastery stage and want to learn to do it themselves.

2 The role of praise

Many will have heard of the feedback sandwich: a directive sandwiched between two positive statements. We all like praise, and often we seek confirmation that we are a good people. It helps our motivation, and makes us feel good about ourselves even if what we did was not right or good enough – we know the maxim of hate the sin but love the sinner. But praise is what we most often recall, and therein lies the dilemma.

Try a feedback sandwich with your child – that is, sandwich the negative or corrective feedback between two pieces of positive feedback. Wait a day so it is not merely short-term memory, and then ask your child what they remembered about the feedback you gave them yesterday. Of course, they will recall the praise when it is the corrective feedback that we want them to recall and act upon. Let's throw away the feedback sandwich, it leads to indigestion.

Our major message here is: Praise given at the same time as feedback more often dilutes the feedback message.

This is NOT saying you should not praise your child – indeed, praise is the essence of building a trusting relationship. It can impel more effort and focus on tasks, and it can reinforce positive attitudes and behavior. But do not confuse praise with feedback, and remember that using the two together is likely to lead to only one (the praise) being heard.

Both of us, John and Kyle, have been to many courses where we were told to increase the amount of feedback we give as teachers, as increasing the quantity of feedback gives more chance that some will hit the mark. But this assumption is wrong. It is less the amount of feedback you *give* and more the amount of feedback that is *received*.

In classes, for example, teachers give an incredible amount of feedback, but so much of it lands nowhere. As with teachers, parents also need to be mindful of how, and how often, feedback is received by children.

The mantra is: Was the feedback heard, was it understood, and was it actionable? If the feedback was actioned, it was great feedback – so reconsider any of your feedback that did not lead to action and wonder how it could have been provided in a way that was heard, understood, and actionable.

Feedback can cost more than it is worth. There can be costs in terms of effort in seeking and then using feedback, and there can be costs in terms of 'face', such as how we look in front of others. There are inference costs relating to misinterpreting the feedback and going down the wrong path. Finally, there can be uncertainty costs in that the child may not be able to cope with ambiguity from feedback or know where to go next. If the costs are too high, it is often more effective to not listen, understand, or use the feedback.

Further, in many instances if a person does not believe they have earned the feedback, they tend to discard it. If the feedback is undeserved, then this can increase negative beliefs of oneself. Feedback is more powerful if it relates to actions that take a lot of effort, where the person wants to reach the success goal, and if the feedback helps them move closer to that goal. At the early stages of performing a task, feedback about effort may spur you to keep investing, but effort feedback at later stages of investment can imply it is not your skills that matter but just time on task.

3 Learning and feedback feed on errors

Feedback is more likely to have a positive impact where there are errors and mistakes than when there is success and correctness. Feedback can lead to improvements and be well received when there is success, but feedback *thrives* on errors, when you are stuck, when you make mistakes, and when you have misconceptions or misunderstandings. Piaget (whom we met in Chapter 6) argued that the key point for any learning is what he called disequilibrium – a gap between what is known and what is not known – and this can be the critical moment for learning to occur. Errors should be seen as opportunities for learning, be a learner's best friend, be seen as exciting and be embraced as the next best thing to advance our learning.

Feedback is most powerful when it addresses faulty interpretations and not a lack of understanding. If the latter, then reteach your children the task. There should be no embarrassment for not knowing or if they do not know what success might look like. Providing feedback will have little effect on performance if the content or tasks you have asked your child to do is unknown, unfamiliar, or abstruse because there will be no hooks on which they can hang, or relate, the feedback you are giving them.

Clearly feedback is part of the learning process, coming after initial instruction, with information provided regarding some aspect of the child's performance. But feedback is of little use if the child has found the initial teaching too hard to understand. Hence, it is vitally important for the child to be able to say they don't understand.

However, there can be a cost with errors, as they can lead to embarrassment, ridicule (especially from peers and siblings), cover-ups, learning to fear failure, and lowered self-esteem. The brain is a great detector of error and can lead to fight or flight – fight the messenger giving the feedback or fly away from it and not hear it, not continue on the task, or do that task again.

This is why building a relationship of trust between you and your children and among the siblings is critical to ensuring children get the most benefit they can from feedback you give based on errors they've made. Such feedback needs to thrive in a risk-free zone for the child, where they can provide conjectures and ideas rather than fully formed thoughts or talk about their feelings when they do not know the right answer. The climate for receiving feedback needs to be one where the consequence of acting on feedback is positive, not negative, for the child.

One worthwhile strategy is to wait before correcting, and instead promote discussion such that the child will come to see the error, and see error detection and improvement as aligned. However, do not be overly sensitive about protecting the child's self-esteem such that you don't correct errors at all. For example, in classrooms when a student makes an error in front of their peers, teachers only use the error 5–10% of the time to advance learning.[2] The rest of the time the teacher simply corrects the error or gets another student to correct it or simply ignores it. What a missed opportunity for improvement. What a powerful message that getting it right is the only answer. No wonder the only kids who put their hand up are those who know the right answer. Students get so many messages that tell them 'smart' means knowing the answer and not making mistakes and that it is best to not invest unless you have a high chance of getting it right, completed on time, and neat. Sad.

A study by Gabriele Steuer and colleagues[3] looked at the impact of 'mistakes friendly' classrooms and 'mistakes unfriendly' classrooms. It found that when students perceived their classroom as mistake-friendly, they increased their effort in their learning. It is the same in families. When there is a sense of safety that a home is a place where is okay to make mistakes, they will not be punished for being wrong then learning can flourish. Consider the opposite – mistakes are punished, perfection is sought – why would you take a risk to learn anything new, difficult, or be creative in seeking more effective ways to complete tasks – you are at risk of punishment, denigration, and shame.

Remember the message about praise – provide the feedback to help the child know where and how to go next, without giving praise or criticism. This will reduce the negative impact on self-esteem and can turn your child into a learner.

So, before you give feedback, make sure that the goal and standards of the task are as clear as possible. Then make sure your feedback helps your child move from where they are toward that goal. Do not include praise, nor include negative comments about them as 'people', as this may lead to them disregarding the feedback. Feedback thrives on errors, provided there is a high-trust, no-blame environment. At all times be mindful of how the feedback is received.

Concluding comments

Feedback is effective when it (1) clarifies success, (2) informs the learner of progress relative to success, (3) offers guidance about the next steps to improve, (4) when it is not mixed with praise, (5) is given and received in a high-trust environment, and (6) when it is heard, understood, and actionable.

Notes

1 Hattie, J., & Clarke, S. (2018). *Visible learning: Feedback*. Routledge.
2 Tulis, M. (2013). Error management behavior in classrooms: Teachers' responses to student mistakes. *Teacher Education, 33*, 56–68. doi:10.1016/j.tate.2013.02.003
3 Steuer, G., Rosentritt-Brunn, G., & Dresel, M. (2013). Dealing with errors in mathematics classrooms: Structure and relevance of perceived error-climate. *Contemporary Educational Psychology, 38*(3), 196–210.

Learning and schooling

7

I am a parent, not a teacher

1 *You are a parent, not a school teacher*

- You are not a school teacher. Understand the boundaries, learn role clarity between being a parent and being a teacher, trust (but verify) the impact of your children's teachers, and love your kids.

- Homework is schoolwork done at home. If there is a problem, it is a school, not a parent, problem.

- Help your child develop friends at school and at home.

2 *Developing the language of learning*

- Parents need to learn the language of learning so that they can better understand what/how they children are doing at school.

- Thus, parents need to know how to talk to teachers and how to raise questions about their children's learning.

3 *How to choose a school*

- Ask what learning, language, and number skills your child will learn: The answers you are looking for are for learning, talking aloud about how they are thinking; for reading, learning concepts about print; and for number skills, patterning and ordination.

- Ask about the rules of engagement: Younger children are rule-governed as it brings structure to their world and helps them fit in.

- Choosing a school is nowhere near as critical as choosing a teacher – but schools are set up to ensure parents never have this choice.

- Ask kids already in the school whether their teachers inspire them and have high expectations for their success.

DOI: 10.4324/9781003257028-10

This chapter demands that parents have clarification about their role as a parent and that this does not include the role of a school teacher. Both parent and teacher, however, aim to develop the language of learning. There are skills in choosing pre-schools and schools and how to learn more about the teacher's understanding of your child.

1 You are a parent, not a school teacher

Schooling was made compulsory in the 1800s based on a simple premise – experts (teachers) are more able to educate children in school-related topics than most parents can. And this has proved to be the case for 150 or so years since.

This is not saying parents are not able to teach their children many things – of course they can, do, and will continue to be most influential. But school learning requires specific skills to teach reading, numeracy, differential equations, filtrations, 5/4 rhythm in jazz, and so much more. Look through any country's curriculum and it is soon overwhelming and outside the skills of most parents – even though many parents were exposed to this same curriculum.

Also, one skill often eludes adults: Adults forget how to think like a novice while still being an expert at knowing the subject matter – and this is a major skill of teachers. No teacher ever says, 'It is easy, it is obvious', as for a novice it is not at all obvious or easy. Teachers have long debated the best scope and sequence to teach ideas; know how to motivate, assess, and evaluate; and are great at knowing how a child got something wrong so as to put them back on the right track. Such expertise is hard earned and requires many years of training, and teachers do it every day with 20–30 children at once.

So: You are not a school teacher. Understand the boundaries, be clear on the differing roles of parent and teacher, trust (but verify) the impact of your children's teachers, and love your kids.

One of the best predictors of success at school is whether your child makes a friend in the first month. Friendship plays an important role in the development of your child's personal competence, identity, and can have long-term positive effects on how they interact with others, have respect for others, and have respect for themselves. Through friends they practice social support and social skills and learn how to empathize and how to deal with conflict resolution.

Friendship groups can become intense social hubs, developing a willingness to share and cooperate. Children learn social norms and can use friendships to challenge the boundaries of social norms. Friendships can lead to greater productivity in tasks and activities.

They are gender differences in patterns of friendship. Boys tend to have more interactions that are activity-based (such as sport) and to interact with multiple participants on social media. Girls are inclined to be more exclusive in their friendships, more likely to base them on intimacy and disclosure of personal thoughts and feelings, and more likely to interact in pairs or small groups of friends. For boys, friendship change can be often related to changes in the membership of these group activities, and for girls, change can happen when they perceive a violation of friendship norms. The message is to work hard to make your child's friendship groups as diverse as possible to ensure that the pool of friends is not just 'like them'; this is a good practice in teaching your child to welcome difference and diversity.

Friendships can be unstable until adolescence, and we have already seen the power friends have in enhancing reputation for adolescents (Chapter 4). In adolescence, about 50–80% of friendships remain intact more than a year and increase in length until they leave high school.

The parent's task is to encourage your child to talk about their friends, encourage them to invite friends for home play, consider extracurricular activities to widen friendship groups, discuss what are and what are not secret messages (such messages can lead to bullying), encourage many friends (friendship at younger ages can be fickle, but losing best friends when older can be traumatic and often not discussed with parents). During adolescence, knowing your teen's friends is among the more insightful ways to know your child. They do not, typically, want you to interact with their friends, but this should not stop knowing them.

Homework is a subject that raises temperatures as parents struggle to find ways to ensure (a) they know there is homework and (b) the child completes the homework.

The effects of homework on achievement in elementary school are close to zero but increase in high school. The reasons for this difference are important – too much homework in elementary school involves children at home learning new ideas whereas in high school it is more about the practice of something already taught at school. If your child cannot do the homework, the worst thing is to do it for them or to make them do it when they do not know how. It is better to communicate to the teacher that your child does not know how to do the homework. Remember, homework is schoolwork done at home, so if it is not working at home, invite the teacher to deal with the issues. It would be wonderful if all homework was a chance to practice what has been already taught, and if only teachers realized the importance of such practice. The worst form of homework is a project – as it so often requires knowledge not yet taught at school and thus depends on parents to provide this project information.

> KH went to elementary school in North Carolina, where every year there was the dreaded science project, and the school's best projects were entered into the NC Science Fair Competition. And then along comes the Monday morning, when KH says, 'Dad, my science project is due this Friday'. 'But', Dad screams, 'you had 6 months and you leave it to the last week, and have no idea what you are going to do. . . .' Fortunately, American commerce is aware of the iniquitousness of science project, so there are whole stores dedicated to providing the materials. That night Dad goes to Michaels and buys the material needed for the volcano, assembles it (Kyle don't touch that, let me do it to get it done), and on Friday Kyle proudly walks into school with his volcano.
>
> What did Kyle learn about science – that it is a drag, that it is about copying some facts from Google, that it is about watching his dad construct a monstrous-looking prop, and that science is little fun.

2 Developing the language of learning

When your child starts school, this is the start of them learning that which they would not learn if they did not go to school. Here is when you start thinking about your role as a parent, not a school-teacher.

As a citizen and voter, you have a say over the curriculum that is taught in schools through the ballot box. Discussing with your child your critique or defense of the curricula is not the best move and certainly saying you did not like x opens permission for them also to not x (especially when x is 'math'). There are perennial debates about the crowded curriculum, with committees formed to do something about it. We have yet to meet a group of adults who cannot shove even more into the curriculum under the name of streamlining, reducing, or modernizing the curriculum.

If you placed the curricula from most Western countries on a table you would find little agreement about when and what to teach.

This is why we claim there is no such notion as 'essential knowledge' that all kids must know; how can there be when every curriculum has different combinations and order?

Most likely, if you were asked to think back to what you learned in English or math or science when you were 10 years, it would be a struggle for you to remember much of it – so do not be overly worried if your child does not get what schools see as 'essential' knowledge – most of it can come later. However, there is one major exception, and that is learning the basics of reading and numeracy by age 8. Any child who has not learned these basics by age 8 is highly likely to be left behind as schools move from learning to read to reading to learn (see Chapter 10).

Note also that nearly all curricula are developed with little to no reference to how kids learn or to the sequence and progressions they make – we know this because there is hardly any research on this. Instead, children are monitored through the scope and sequence of learning as outlined by adults, and if a child does not conform or grow to the adults' notions, it is the child who is blamed and classified.

Learning progressions should be seen like a GPS.[1] As we've noted before, there are multiple routes to success and different times needed to reach that success, in the same way there are multiple ways to drive from Sydney to Melbourne (or Boston to New York, Leeds to London), with different travel times to reach the destination: Most people will travel the Hume Highway, but some will travel the coast road, some will go inland, and many will deviate and see the sights. There is no right way to reach a successful destination, so if your child travels a different road from the majority of children, this is not necessarily a problem.

We evaluated major initiatives to raise achievement in five schools in the lowest socioeconomic area of New Zealand[2] (see also the Appendix). There were many initiatives over the three years, and one stood out. This was the early 2000s when many homes did not have access to computers, so computers were provided for the parents on the assumption that they and their children would learn and do the homework together. The project employed ex-teachers to go to the homes to teach the parents how to use the computer and the internet. We found it was not computers that were making a positive difference to student learning but the presence of the ex-teachers. The parents were learning how to talk to teachers, how to raise questions about what they didn't know, what their children didn't know, and how to improve their, and their children's, learning. More parents then came to school meetings, and went to the school, and wanted to talk to the teachers – the initiative had generated a language of learning in the home. The parents became more aware of ways their children were learning, the value of the 'struggle' of learning, that learning is hard work, and the worth of learning different strategies of learning. This is learning about learning. We called our final report 'When Parents Learn the Language of Learning'.

During COVID this learning about learning has been one of the wonderful realizations. For parents it is not 'Is my child above average, and do they behave at school?' but it is seeing that learning is a desirable struggle, that not knowing is an opportunity, that there are multiple ways to learn when you are a novice, that kids learn with and through each other, and that children can become motivated to learn schoolwork. While we argue that it is the role of teachers to orchestrate this motivation, learning, and progressions, it is the parents' role to reinforce, model, and welcome the learning.

It is this talking about learning in the home that is all powerful – much more so than doing homework, adding more programs for your child to go to after school, or finding websites and apps to promote school knowledge. Your role is more to do with the conditions and resources for learning than the content. What does your child do when they do not know the key question to ask, are they receptive to feedback, and do they see failure as their best friend? At the dinner table, talk about learning and desirable struggle and never about 'What did you learn today?' Ban the 'what' and embrace the 'how' of learning. This is what we mean by the 'language of learning'.

3 How to choose a school

A probable topic of many dinner conversations among you and your friends is what school should the children go to. In reality, most times the school chooses you as it is the neighborhood school. Sean Leaver[3] outlined reasons why choosing a school is a 'wicked' problem, that is, a problem that is difficult to solve because there are incomplete, contradictory, and sometimes changing requirements that are often difficult to recognize. A definitive judgment about the choice can only really be made with hindsight, given the long time frames needed to know if you have made a 'right' decision, one choice is made it is very hard to go back and 'unmake' them, your child's interaction and experience in the chosen school is unique, choices of the school typically involve 'values' (e.g., academic pressure, encouraging, sup-porting, discipline, and convenience), and there can be conflicting views of values across parents and by your child; often the best infor-mation on which to base a decision is hot knowledge or the grape-vine,[4] and parents do not have the option to make a 'wrong' choice when made on behalf of their children. Given this wickedness, many parents are risk-averse, looking for schools with many options and resources, thus increasing the likelihood of optimal matching of their child's needs. Once a choice is made, parents can then seek confir-mation evidence that their choice was right (the Ikea effect, we love the cabinet we made because we made it).

But let us start with pre-school as that is becoming all the more important for some as the pressure is mounted to give your child the 'best start'.

Should I send my child to a pre-school setting?

Should you send your child to pre-school or not? The E4Kids proj-ect is one of the largest studies of pre-school settings – it followed children age 3-plus in more than 3,000 early childcare settings over five years. These care centers were publicly funded kindergartens, private ventures, and home care settings. Over all the types of care settings, on a scale from 1 to 10, they score a 7–8 for their devel-opment of emotional and social development, but only a 2–3 for learning development. Worse, there are fewer quality care settings in lower socio-economic areas so they have a double whammy – fewer resources in the home and fewer quality childcare settings. Indeed, childcare settings in lower socio economic areas were weakest on instructional support – and this despite knowing about the impor-tance of learning development in these early years. Where quality care does occur, it can make enormous differences.

There have been 44 meta-analyses of the effects of preschool, based on close to a million students.[5] The difference between home care in someone else's home and full day care is small ($d = 0.12$), and between half- and full-day kindergarten is also small ($d = 0.18$). It is not the site that matters much. The effect on learning of pre-school over staying at home hovers between 0.25–0.40 on aver-age but goes up much more for pre-schools with at-risk students ($d = 0.56$). By age 8, it is hard to see much difference between those who did and did not go to a pre-school – although the effects are more marked for those who start far behind their peers in their skills in learning, and as we noted when discussing the Matthew effect, these early differences can quickly magnify.

Developing the fundamentals of learning in these early years is through the development of language. Iram Siraj-Blatchford and colleagues[6] identified four major features of quality early childcare settings for parents to look for. First was the nature and quality of adult–child interactions. Quality interactions involve the adults listening and interacting with the child, modeling how to do things, appropriately 'stretching' the child's thinking, and asking the child open-ended, not closed, questions (which occurred less than 5% of the time).

Second, quality childcare settings are those that have good processes to assess a child's current stage of development, know the steps needed to move the child forward, and know how to evaluate the child's progress. So as a parent, ask the childcare workers what and how they know of your child's development and the steps they are taking to further that development.

Third, a quality childcare setting will share its ideas, aims, and practices with you as parents so that the learning occurs both at school and in the childcare setting.

Fourth, quality childcare settings have clear behavior and discipline policies which include staff talking through conflicts with children, supporting children's development of social skills, and ensuring any misbehavior is not ignored.

There are many excellent policy documents in the early years. Take the Australian state of Victoria, which has the 'Early Years Learning and Development Framework 0–8'.[7] The framework document outlines five major outcomes for early childhood programs:

- Children have a strong sense of identity (identity)
- Children are connected with and contribute to their world (community)
- Children have a strong sense of wellbeing (wellbeing)
- Children are confident and involved learners (learning)
- Children are effective communicators (communication)

The latter two are most appropriate for our theme about learning. From 0–8 years, children 'learn how to learn' and to 'make decisions and choices, to influence events and to have an impact on their world'. They learn that learning is exploratory, fun, and rewarding.

They learn to share feelings and thoughts about learning from others. And they learn about gaining meaning from books and other media and sharing the enjoyment of language in a variety of ways.

The document is specific about the skills and understandings that need to be developed by parents and educators over these years. For example,

- children interact verbally and nonverbally with others for a range of purposes;

- children engage with a range of texts and get meaning from these texts;

- children express ideas and make meaning using a range of media;

- children begin to understand how symbols and pattern systems work; and

- children use information and communication technologies to access information, investigate ideas, and represent their thinking.

It's worth checking out policy documents such as this for the detailed information they provide about what's involved in learning in these early years.

We all know the power of reading to young children – it broadens their vocabulary, makes them interested in the fun of reading, develops their listening skills, and intrigues their imagination. Less attention has been given to the power of numbers, although presenting numbers to young children is just as important. From a very early age, young children are aware of mathematical elements in their environment.[8] That is, they think and behave mathematically, particularly in the core skill of seeing patterns such as repetition, spatial relations, sorting, and copying and extending patterns. You should identify and talk to your child about what they are doing, extend them, and provide games and tasks that enhance their language about patterning.

Choosing an early childhood setting

When deciding on a setting, first ask the staff about what they see as the aim of learning in this setting for your child. In Iram Siraj-Blatchford's study, many child minders were bemused by this question and, when prompted, talked about wanting children to be happy, enjoy coming, and have fun. While these are all important, more is needed. Listen for clues about children playing together, talking about what they are doing, learning to listen to others about their interpretations, learning right from wrong, working through conflict, seeing errors, and not knowing and failure as being a learner's best friend. These are all great skills that assist learning. Ask the child minders how they record, and inform you about, your child's progress, especially their progress in language. Ask the staff how they 'teach' your child in this setting (e.g., Do you plan for their learning? How do you know they have succeeded? How do you record this learning [so I can share it]?). If the staff shun the notion of teaching, run a mile. That 'teaching' is not that of a Year 1–7 teacher, but nonetheless, there are skills that need to be intentionally taught.

Here are eight simple guidelines:

1 Count the words you hear in various pre-school settings and in your home, and place the child with the one with the greatest number of words.

2 Ask who initiates the learning activities: If they say the child, run a mile; if they say the teacher, run an extra mile; if they say both, keep asking more questions.

3 Ask, 'What do you teach my child?' – if the answer is reading and numeracy, lose interest. If the answer is language, language, language, which helps in understanding concepts about print and order of numbers, and if they talk about developing gross and fine motor skills, stay tuned.

4 Ask about the educational experience of the teachers. If there are no qualified teachers, get out fast.

5 Ask, 'My child is x years old. What learning activities would be appropriate?' If they answer too quickly, be careful; if they say, 'I will have to work with your child to find out', these are soothing words to hear.

6 Childcare settings are usually good for social and emotional learning (ask some other parents about this), but the discriminator is cognitive learning. Ask: 'What do you do here to develop my child's cognitive learning?'

7 Observe what the children at the childcare setting doing – watch the kids, not the adults. Do they look busy or bored? Are they interacting with others? Are the activities all prescribed, or are there many different things to do and choose from? Count the books.

8 Ask the other parents about the center – ask, 'And what is your child learning here?' Can you give me some examples? You do not want to hear, 'They learn to read and write', but 'They learn new words and how to talk about what they are doing'.

Then there are considerations for transitioning into school – and again the question is, How to choose a school? The first question parents often ask, is whether my child is ready for school. But it is not whether your child is 'ready' for school but more whether the school is ready for your child. There is no magic age for starting school. There's no easy answer to the question, 'Who decided that five was the right age to start school'. In 1876, the then British prime minister Benjamin Disraeli wanted five years of compulsory schooling, but the business and parent sectors were adamant that children should be in work by age 10 – hence, they agreed to start schooling at age 5. These days, most children start school at 5 or 6 (although it ranges from 3 in France and Hungary to 7 years in Scandinavian countries). However, a more difficult question is about when a 5-year-old should start – the new academic year after they turn 5? The term after they turn 5? Or the day they turn 5? The closer the policy is to the latter, the more effective it is.

Consider the school year after the child turns 5 – you will get children with a year's gap in age, which is one year's extra life experience. No wonder relative age within a class has a big effect on later achievement. If the policy is the day after they turn 5, this would usually be coupled with policies of transition classes, with some moving up earlier to the next level than others.

Not surprisingly, age is correlated with achievement in these early years – early starters benefit compared to later starters.[9] The core issue, however, is less to do with *when* a child starts as it is with *what happens* when they start school. The emphasis needs to be on developing the child's sense of social responsibility and their skills at working with others, their skills about concepts about print, number, and patterning (noted earlier) as these are the key components for learning to read and becoming numerate.[10]

Graver Whitehurst and Christopher Lonigan[11] showed that 'children's ability to demonstrate simple knowledge of print (knowing letter names), phonological awareness (being able to rhyme), and writing (printing their own name), at the end of the pre-school year was a good predictor of reading performance at the end of the first grade (age six)'. If your child enters school without these skills, and if they are not then systematically taught these skills, they will struggle with reading and mathematics. Also, for children without these skills, the sooner they start school, the better for them.

Note the critical difference between the fundamental concepts about reading and numeracy (pre-school years) and the skills to read and do mathematics (the school years). In pre-school, children spend proportionally more time on tasks of their choice whereas in school teachers take more control of this choice and students are more passive. At pre-school, the concepts and understanding are more embedded in activities compared to more subject-related focus in schools. These differences are not accidental and do not mean one is right and one is wrong.

When starting school, children enter a complex, unfamiliar world, have fewer choices, are asked to engage in structured timelines, and explore new ideas. And they have a high need to make friends quickly. This is why orientation programs can be so powerful, although they tend to be far too short (too often offered in an hour or two). When interviewing these young explorers of the new world, Sue Dockett and Bob Perry[12] remind us that 5–6-year-old children are rule-governed, and their focus on rules provides them cues as to what schools and classrooms mean to them. Teachers see it as social adjustment, kids see it as learning rules – for them, it is all about fitting in.

They are asked to learn the rules of engagement, work with others and engage with the teacher; they see it as compliance, acknowledging the power of the teacher. They learn that getting it right and knowing the answer is the game here, and if they are unsure, they begin to distance themselves from the enjoyment of learning and school. They begin to see fairness as important – Why does that child get away with breaking the rules? Why is that child favored by the teacher? Why do the big kids seem to live by different rules? School can be a scary, weird, lonely place where children soon learn whether or not they are one of the winners. School can be seen as a place where the adult controls the learning, tells you what to do, and transmits the skills of learning – no surprise that these young children see the best learners as the most compliant, the ones who already know a lot and who listen most to the teacher.

In the teaching to read in the first year, there is more coloring in and pasting than specific learning of the skills of reading.[13] The early years of school which are often a sharp break from the more free-flowing, choice-dominant, friendship-rich early childhood settings.

Parents can help by listening to their child's thoughts, worries, and successes in learning in the class, and help them understand the rules and their consequences.

Sue Docket and Bob Perry[14] have the following worthwhile recommendations for starting school:

- Talk with your children, taking time to listen to issues that are of concern or interest for them. Often, issues that cause anxiety can be rectified quite easily by a knowing adult.

- Recognize that children may not interpret contexts in the same ways as adults. Hence, what adults think their children are doing may be interpreted quite differently by children.

- Discuss any rules with children, rather than imposing rules. Children can be involved in identifying rules that may be necessary and setting.

- Discuss appropriate consequences for breaking the rules.

- Encourage children to question, as well as to respect, rules.

- Recognize the transition to school as a significant time of change for many children.

It is less 'Is your child ready for school?' as it is 'Has your child developed sufficient social and emotional maturity to cope with others, understand rules and consequences, attend to learning tasks, have the fundamental skills about concepts about print and patterning, and have the ability to make friends?' – the very skills that need to be the focus of the first five years. In an impressive study on these specific attributes, Greg Duncan and colleagues[15] found that the best predictors of later achievement, in order, were school-entry mathematics (knowledge of numbers, ordinality), reading (vocabulary, knowing letters, words, beginning and ending word sounds), and attention (task persistence, lack of impulsivity, control, sustain attention).

Choosing an elementary/primary school

Here's the reality – choosing a school is nowhere as critical as choosing a teacher. However, schools are set up in a way that ensures parents never have the choice of choosing a teacher. Even as educators 'in the know', we only succeeded once in this quest – John said to the principal, 'The eldest child had Ms X and she messed him up, the middle child had Ms X and she messed him up also, so give me a break with the third'. The third child got the second-worst teacher in that school, so judge for yourself how successful we really were. The greatest source of variability is not the variability across schools, but the variability within a school. But you have few, in any, powers to choose the teacher. This is why the advice about choosing schools is more critical – looking at the culture of learning, asking students whatever the grade what they think is a great learner at this school, asking whether the school is an inviting place to come to learn, and inquiring 'what happens in this school when a student makes a mistake, does not know, and wants to seek help with their learning. Listen carefully.

This in-school variability is why it is unwise to change schools in a search for the magic elixir, as you may get the teacher of choice in one year but after that, it is quasi-random. We want every teacher to be great – our Visible Learning motto is *Great teachers by design, not by chance*. A major aim of the Visible Learning professional development is geared directly to scaling up the effectiveness of *all* teachers so they *all* have a high impact.

Let us make a bold statement that may help. We do not care less about how a teacher teaches – there is far too much debate about how to teach, the styles of teaching, a teacher's right to have the autonomy to teach their way, and so on. We do not care about how they teach; what we care about is the impact of their teaching. Our research has shown that impact is the biggest issue in the education system that it's possible to have any control over. The question to ask the teacher is. 'What impact do you as a teacher expect to have on my child?' Also, talk to parents of children who have had the teacher and ask them, 'What impact has this teacher had on your child?' And even better, ask this question of the children who've been taught by the teacher.

Impact does not necessarily mean the teacher led the child to pass the tests, to gain high achievement. This is a very narrow measure, and sometimes 'high achievement' is not good enough and can indeed be misleading. Impact also refers to turning your child on to the passion of learning, no matter where they start. Teacher impact means developing in children the skills and confidence to work in teams and for the children to want to come to class because they have a sense of belonging in the class and school. It means developing children's ability to learn to think and evaluate their own learning progress and to build respect for self and respect for others.

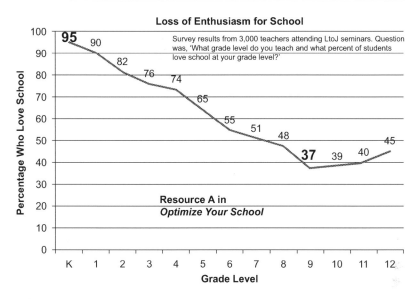

FIGURE 7.1 Jenkin's curve relating the percentage of students who like coming to school to learn across grades. Republished with permission of Corwin Press, from *Optimize Your School*, Lee Jenkins, 2016; permission conveyed through Copyright Clearance Center, Inc.

When considering choosing a school, remember the Jenkins curve. Lee Jenkins[16] has an aim to create the perfect school. Lee asks teachers, 'What percent of students at your grade love school?' Simple, yes, but the findings are scary. Almost all (95%) of K–1 students are seen to love school, but this dips too, at best, four out of ten students by the start of high school (Figure 7.1). Is your child one of these six out of ten who do not see schools as inviting and as developing their love the learning? While they may like school for friends, sport, and social life, it is important that they also like school for learning. We implore school leaders to 'beat the Jenkins curve'. When Lee asks high school students if they love learning at school, the answers are usually that less than 10% do. The loss of joyful school learning begins in kindergarten and Grade 1. Lee's mission is to create and esteem schools that beat his curve. Such schools are out there, and there are many of them. We hope your child finds one – or at least you find school leaders who know if their school beats the Jenkins curve.

Consider these ten indicators for recognizing a good school:

1   In the playground, do the students look each other in the eye? Or do they avoid each other or sit in cliques.?

2 Diversity breeds fresh thinking. Can the school show you genuine evidence diversity is encouraged?

3 How does the school measure success? By the achievements of the few or the many? By only test scores, or do they know and understand the importance of ensuring students want to come to school to learn (they know about the Jenkins curve)?

4 Ask to meet the best teacher. If the school leaders tell you all the teachers are good, they're not thinking clearly.

5 Who do students turn to? Every student should have someone who knows how they are doing and will spend time with them.

6 Do new students make friends in the first month? (Ask some parents of older kids). It is a critical indicator for success: How does the school make sure it happens with all students?

7 Does the school like mistakes? Learning starts from not knowing, so does the school embrace that? Do students feel confident enough to talk about errors or not knowing something? Ask children in the class: 'What do you do when you do not know?' If they say they ask the teacher or put up their hand, be unimpressed.

8 Are students 'assessment capable' in this school? Can they talk about how well they are doing, where they are at now, and where, learning-wise, they are going to next?

9 Does the school use acceleration for all? Are students enabled to learn at different speeds?

10 What feedback do students get? Ask the children: 'What feedback did you receive about your schoolwork today?'

Then there are the 'meet the teacher' moments. These may be student-led conferences, where your child provides 20–30 minutes of reporting on their progress. This approach works best (and typically only works) when the teacher deliberately teaches self-regulation, engages in releasing responsibility of teaching to the student, teaches students about their learning strategies and success criteria, and provides high levels of feedback. The other end of the 'meet the teacher' scale is the dreaded ten minutes with each teacher in a crowded gymnasium. Oh, how we hated these sessions, with the teacher flipping through their notes to remind them which child is yours. Our message is simple – these sessions are for the teacher to inform you of your child's progress, behavior, and the likelihood of success in the class. if the progress is not satisfactory, ask what the teacher intends to do about it.

John worked with Roger Peddie[17] to analyze school reports from more than 300 students – the sort of reports that are sent home once or twice a year. On the basis of these reports, 98% of students were achieving well, putting in an effort, and a pleasure to teach. All lies, and a public relations disaster. During COVID, parents had greater insight into their child's learning at school than ever, and we hope schools remember this and run student-led conferences, video some distance learning classes (at school but send them home), and remove those woefully misleading school reports.

A parent emailed us about how to approach parent–teacher interviews, and we responded. He gave the questions to the teacher before the meeting and was careful to not be over zealous and upset the teachers – and after the meeting refined them. Here is what we asked:

We're looking forward to hearing about how Kyle is going. Here are some questions regarding his learning we would like to work through with you at the interview:

1 Where is Kyle doing well (strengths) at the moment? And where do you expect him to be up to in 3 months from now with this strength?
2 Where is Kyle struggling (weaknesses) at the moment?

    a Of these learning struggles, what are you doing about these and how would we know as parents that he is mastering what is required of him?
    b If you could pick one area to focus on improving this struggle for Kyle, what would it be?

3 Where should Kyle be at now with his reading?

    a Is Kyle on grade level for reading? If so, how does he rank among the Grade 1 cohort precisely? That is, 5th? 15th? 50th?
    b Do you know what his reading goals are? Does he feel he can exceed them? Please elaborate.
    c What about math, science, and writing? Can you elaborate on his performance? What is he doing well at? And not well?

> d What does Kyle need to learn next across math, science, and writing in order to improve?
>
> 4 Based on Kyle's student report results from Semester 1 and 2 last year, do you feel that his overall academic progress this term is trending the same, above, or below his previous results?
>
> a If you think Kyle is likely to achieve the same results or worse than last year in any key subject, what are you doing about this and what can we do to help?
>
> 5 Is Kyle engaged and enjoying learning? Is Kyle happy?
>
> a How does Kyle contribute to the class atmosphere?
> b From spending time with him, which motivation or teaching techniques motivate Kyle the most? Can you elaborate or share an example?
>
> 6 Who are his friends in class and who does he like to work with?
> 7 What question should we have asked you about Kyle that we have missed?
> 8 From your perspective, what does Kyle need to learn or change to become an outstanding Year 1 student? Can you give an example of how he could exceed your current expectations?
> 9 Do you have any final concerns about Kyle?

Concluding comments

You are not a school teacher, and your major role is to advance the skills of learning – showing alternative ways of resolving conflicts, solving problems, and working with others. You retain many teaching roles in the home about social and emotional learning, developing your child's self-respect and respect for others. You need to work hard to help your child from becoming lonely and instead support friendships.

Choosing early childhood settings is to choose the most language-rich setting. At home, talk about the learning at school (less 'what did you do at school' and more 'tell us about your learning today'). Establish routines for homework, but you are not the homework police. If your child is struggling with homework or schoolwork, esteem the struggle and teach them strategies to seek help. Learning is hard work. Recall a major lesson from COVID teaching – you have 1–2 school-age children, but your teacher has 20–30 (or in high school up to 200) children a day for 200 days a year. They are the experts in motivation, learning, and evaluating schoolwork – appeal to them for advice. Work on the questions you want to ask teachers and never disparage a teacher as this is infectious and a great way to turn your child off schoolwork (and they work with this teacher 5–6 hours a day).

Notes

1 Cawsey AM, C., Hattie, J., & Masters AO, G. N. (2019). *Growth to achievement: On-demand resources for teachers.* https://research.acer.edu.au/monitoring_learning/39/

2 Clinton, J., Hattie, J., & Dixon, R. (2007). *Evaluation of the Flaxmere Project: When families learn the language of school.* Ministry of Education.

3 Leaver, S. (2019). *How parents solve the 'wicked' problem of choosing a school: A qualitative investigation within a behavioural economics framework.* Paper presented at RMIT Conference, Sydney, Australia.

4 Ball, S. J., & Vincent, C. (1998). 'I Heard It on the Grapevine': 'hot' knowledge and school choice. *British Journal of Sociology of Education, 19*(3), 377–400.

5 See www.visiblelearningmetax.com.

6 Siraj-Blatchford, I., Muttock, S., Sylva, K., Gilden, R., & Bell, D. (2002). *Researching effective pedagogy in the early years.* Institute of London Research Report RR356.

7 www.education.vic.gov.au/childhood/professionals/learning/Pages/veyldf.aspx

8 Hannula-Sormunen, M. M. (2015). Spontaneous focusing on numerosity and its relation to counting and arithmetic. In *The Oxford handbook of numerical cognition* (pp. 275–290). Oxford University Press.

9 Sharp, C. (2002, November 1). School starting age: European policy and recent research. *When should our children start school.* Paper presented at the LGA Seminar 'When Should Our Children Start School?', LGA Conference Centre, Smith Square, London, United Kingdom. Tymms, P., Merrell, C., & Henderson, B. (2000). Baseline assessment and progress during the first three years at school. *Educational Research and Evaluation, 6*(2), 105–129.

10 Schweinhart, L. J., & Weikart, D. P. (1998). Why curriculum matters in early childhood education. *Educational Leadership, 55*, 57–61.

11 Whitehurst, G. J., & Lonigan, C. J. (1998). Child development and emergent literacy. *Child Development, 69*, 848–872.

12 Dockett, S., & Perry, B. (1999). Starting school: What do the children say? *Early Child Development and Care, 159*(1), 107–119. doi:10.1080/0300443991590109

13 van Hees, J. A. G. (2011). *Oral expression of five and six year olds in low socio-economic schools.* Unpublished doctoral dissertation, University of Auckland.

14 Dockett, S., & Perry, B. (1999). Starting school: What do the children say? *Early Child Development and Care, 159*(1), 107–119. doi:10.1080/0300443991590109

15 Duncan, G. J., Dowsett, C. J., Claessens, A., Magnuson, K., Huston, A. C., Klebanov, P., Pagani, L. S., Feinstein, L., Engel, M., Brooks-Gunn, J., Sexton, H., Duckworth, K., & Japel, C. (2007). School readiness and later achievement. *Developmental Psychology, 43*(6), 1–36, 1428.

16 Jenkins, L. (2015). *Optimize your school: It's all about the strategy.* Corwin Press.

17 Hattie, J. A. C., & Peddie, R. (2003). School reports: "Praising with faint damns". *Set: Research Information for Teachers, 3*, 4–9.

8

I expose my child to language, language, language

1 Language, language, language

- Five-year-old children from more affluent homes are exposed to about 30 million more words than 5-year-old children from less affluent homes.

- You can avoid the Matthew effect (the rich get richer, the poor stay poor) by much talking, listening, and engaging in learning with your child early, often, and positively.

2 The early years need not predict later success

- It's never too late to engage in talking, listening, and learning.

This chapter aims to outline the three major foci of the early years: language, language, and language. It over emphasizes talking and listening, expanding your child's vocabulary and understanding, answering their many 'Why' questions as they aim to make sense of their world.

Language, language, language

In a famous study published in 2003, Betty Hart and Todd Risley[1] followed a group of children from welfare homes, a group from low-resourced families, and a group from well-resourced homes (university professors) over three years, recording everything *done* by the children, *to* them, and *around* them. The three groups of children attended playgroups at early childhood settings, and each group eagerly engaged with a wide variety of materials and language. They all explored new vocabulary, but the developments and speed of increase of language differed between the three groups.

DOI: 10.4324/9781003257028-11

Hart and Risley delved deeper and followed three groups of children and their families over four years, starting when the children were 7–9 months old. This included meeting with the children and their families regularly and recording everything in the home: the language, the play, the interactions. Over 90% of the words recorded by each child were the same words used by their parents, and by 3 years of age, most children were talking and using a similar number of words as their parents. How they talked how much they talked, the style of talk, and the vocabulary growth had been set by about age 3. The children were mimicking their parents.

But still, the Hart and Risley followed the students – indeed 1,300 hours of casual interactions between parents and their children. Figure 8.1

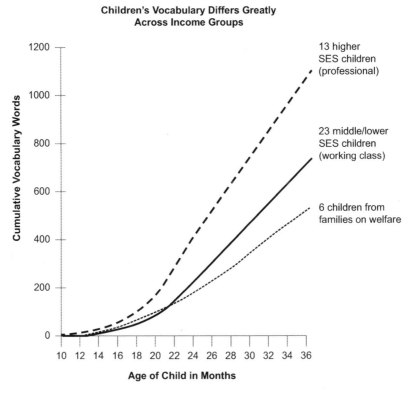

Children's Vocabulary Differs Greatly Across Income Groups

FIGURE 8.1 Growth of vocabulary across income groups.

Hart and Risley (1995), *Meaningful Differences in the Everyday Experience of Young American Children*, Baltimore, Paul H. Brookes Publishing Co., Inc.,: Reprinted by permission.

Note: SES = socioeconomic status.

tells it all – there is indeed a Matthew effect, even at that early age. The growth is much slower in the poorer families and the growth curve is much steeper in the well-resourced families.

The researchers noticed no great difference in the ways the three groups of parents raised their children – all played and talked with them; all disciplined and taught them manners; all provided them with toys and talked about much the same things. Most went to preschool, which made little difference, and certainly the children's performance at age 3 was a good predictor of their language skills at age 9.

Hart and Risley summarized their findings:

> Simply in words heard, the average child on welfare was having half as much experience per hour (616 words per hour) as the average working-class child (1,251 words per hour) and less than one-third that of the average child in a professional family (2,153 words per hour). These relative differences in the amount of experience were so durable over the more than two years of observations that they provide the best basis we currently have for estimating children's actual life experience.

Extrapolating that to 100 hours a week, which is the typical amount of time a child and parent are together, this means that the average child in the professional family has 215,000 words of language experience, the average child in a working-class family has 125,000 words, and the average child in a welfare family has 62,000 words of language experience. In a 5,200-hour year, the amount would be 11.2 million words for a child in a professional family, 6.5 million words for a child in a working-class family, and 3.2 million words for a child in a welfare family. In four years of such experience, an average child in a professional family would have accumulated experience with almost 45 million words – this are not unique words but the number of words they hear including many repetitions. In contrast, an average child in a working-class family would have accumulated experience with 26 million words, and an average child in a welfare family would have accumulated experience with 13 million words. By age 4, the average child in a welfare family might have 13 million fewer words of cumulative experience than the average child in a working-class family. This linear extrapolation is shown in Figure 8.1.

By age 5 there is a 30-million-word gap in the number of words heard by a child in a professional family versus the number a child in a welfare class family has heard.

But there is more.

Hart and Risley found that a child from a well-resourced family accumulates 32 affirmations (encouragements) and five prohibitions (discouragements) over an hour and that a child from a working-class or welfare family has five affirmations and 11 prohibitions per hour. That is a 6:1 versus 1:2 difference. In a year, the professional family child gets 166,000 affirmations to 26,000 prohibitions and the working-class child 26,000 encouragements to 57,000 discouragements. 'By the age of 4, the average child in a welfare family might have had 144,000 fewer encouragements and 84,000 more discouragements of his or her behavior than the average child in a working-class family'.

By age 5, the professional-class child hears the world as a place for encouragement and the working-class child a place for discouragement.

But there is yet even more.

Hart and Risley distinguished between 'business talk' and 'extra talk'. The first gets the work of life done (Come here, put your shoes on, eat your dinner), and the second is the icing on the cake (Look at the sky, this apple is juicy, what's its name?). The welfare and working-class children heard mostly business talk, but the professional-class child also heard the extra talk. It was the continuation of talk beyond the necessary, the verbal back-and-forth between child and adult or older sibling that was so different. This extra 'baby talk' and active talking make the difference. It is not language gained from plonking your child in front of a television or computer game as this is passive language and often not heard by the child. It is the social responsiveness and social interaction that are part of the language that makes the difference. So, talk, talk, talk, listen, listen, listen, engage, engage, engage.

But there is yet even more.

This Matthew effect continues. Max Pfost led a team[2] that synthesized the voluminous amount of evidence on this phenomenon throughout schooling. Their interest was whether students who read better at early ages showed further positive reading literacy gains and those who read poorly showed negative or lesser gains. The answer was yes.

There are many explanations for this:

■ An initial advantage in a certain outcome (such as learning to read) tends to beget further advantages, whereas an initial disadvantage begets further disadvantages.

- Better readers seem to be more motivated to read and hence read more – thus, there is a 'virtuous circle of reading' for the well resourced and a 'vicious circle of nonreading' for the lesser resourced.

- Teachers stop teaching beginning reading by the middle of Grade 2 and find ways for non-readers to engage in school's task without their need to read – so the poorer readers never learn to catch up.

Pfost and colleagues concluded that there is indeed a Matthew effect primarily relating to the core notions of learning to read (i.e., learning the skills of decoding and developing vocabulary).

Dana Suskind and colleagues[3] have written the best book based on the Hart and Risley work – not only rich in evidence but also written in a most engaging style for parents. She recommends three major implications:

Tune in – Notice what the baby is focused on; then talk *with* the child about it. Even if the child is too young to understand, tuning in is the first step to building language. As adults we often switch what we are looking at and doing, and this switching is a learned skill – some of us can do it more easily than others (some parents even have eyes in the back of their heads). This tuning-in is part of building the ability to focus, relate a word to an object, and engage in an activity (in this case, associating a thing with a word). Paul Tough[4] has a similar idea asking caregivers to engage in 'serve and return' behavior – where infants make a sound or look at an object and the parent returns the serve: 'Yes, that is a nice sound, yes that is your doggy'. These serves and returns can be rich in information for the child, helping them make sense of their world. Modeling this listening and talking to the child is powerful, and builds the child's sense that communication and learning is a two-way process. Parents can reduce a child's uncertainty and stressors by behaving in predictable ways. When your child cries and screams, if your response is calmness then the child is more likely to be calmer when under stress; if your response is tense and stressed, the child is more likely to remain tense and stressed (see Chapter 4 on coping strategies).

Talk more – Talking more refers not just to the number of words, but also the kinds of words and how these words are being said. Talk '*with* a child, especially what the child is focusing on, not *to* him or her' (Suskind, p. 143). There is a mutual engagement. Narrate what you are doing; for example, 'I'm going to give you an apple', 'Let me put your shoes on'. Use plenty of pronouns (you, it, he, she) as these are the 'air' of language, and use affirmatives and 'extra talk'. John Medina[5] claims the gold standard is about 2,100 words per hour with an emphasis on feedback words – looking at your infant; imitating their vocalization, laughter, and facial expressions; and rewarding their language attempts with heightened attention. While this may sound like a high number, we typically hear about 100,000 words a day. Medina recommends that parents use the sing-song voice (elongating vowels, higher and exaggerated pitch, melodic tone); over pronounced phonetics, which helps infants hear the sounds); holding the child when talking to them, and reading to them (from 3 months) even if it is talking about the pictures. Medina concludes that talking to babies 'is like fertilizer for neurons' (p. 129). This 'parentese' form of talk gets your child's attention, engages them, and allows them to listen to the sounds more clearly. Naja Ramirez and colleagues[6] showed that such language invokes brain capacity not only in the auditory areas of the brain but also in the centers that are responsible for children's ability to respond to us verbally – even before they can speak. Infants who heard the most 'parentese' each day learned over twice as many words as those who heard standard speech most of the time.

Take turns – Engage your child in a conversation; it is not all one way from you to your child. This, Suskind argues, is the 'gold standard'. For example, the child rubs her eyes and you take your turn, responding, 'Oh, you are feeling sleepy'. As the child gets older, ask 'why' and 'how' questions, but resist asking too many 'what' questions as that often leads to single-word or short-phrase answers, and cuts off the turn taking.

As with all academic papers, there are arguments about the Hart and Risley study, but it certainly has raised major issues about the importance of language, encouragement, and active talk. It also means we should start early to ensure we put the child on to the fast track to hear more language, and it should be unforgivable if a child is not taught to read by the age of 8.

Ken Blaiklock[7] watched the interaction between parents where the baby was placed in prams or buggies facing forward to see the world (the majority), and when the baby was facing the parent. He noted the very low incidence of parent – child talk (about 10%) in all cases, and, confirming a previous study by Suzanne Zeedyk,[8] found parents were interacting with their children twice as much when the child was facing the parents rather than facing forward.

The message is simple – start talking, listening, and engaging in language with your child early, often, and positively.

2 The early years need not predict later success

There are many claims about the power of the early years to predict later success in school. There are two major problems with this argument.

First, if correct, this would mean those who struggle in the early years have higher probabilities of being doomed later on; you then have to seriously question the role of schools. Surely the role of schools is to mess up, for the betterment of all, any high correlation between early years and school outcomes. Some schools are brilliant at doing this, whereas others accept the correlational fate and offer many reasons for why some students cannot achieve.

Second, the evidence is not that supportive of a high correlation; the relationship is more modest. If there is a high correlation, then we need to ensure every pre-school child goes to a wonderful pre-school. By age 8, however, it can be hard to identify which students went to a pre-school or not. Too many pre-schools are not that wonderful at doing the best possible job of developing learning in pre-schoolers. Too many pre-schools shun notions of learning the fundamentals of reading and numeracy, by which we mean exposing children to concepts about print and counting numbers – not teaching them to read or do sums.

We analyzed many thousands of 5-year-old children who completed a battery of entrance to school measures as they started school.[9]

These measures included concepts about print, oral language, and a sense of number. There were about 5–8% who had such low scores that their chances of catching up were bleak. Take the first item on concepts about print – give a child a book upside down and ask them to turn to the first page. One out of 12 children did not know to turn the book around before opening – and many had been to pre-school. Further, when you ask teachers to identify at age 5 those students who are unlikely to reach fundamental levels of literacy and numeracy at age 8, they are very accurate. So given these students can be identified, why is something not done to help them? The best estimate is that, on average, there are 4–5 of these students in every elementary school – teachers need to put faces and actions to these children immediately. No child should be lacking adequate reading and number skills by age 8 (when most classes are well past teaching the basics of these subjects); if they do lack the skills at age 8, the Matthew effect shows they will continue to struggle. Make sure your child is not in this category. And if so, then much work is needed to provide additional teaching to catch up as soon as possible. This is the major reason for attending to the skills we have outlined and have emphasized the importance of language, language, and language in the early years.

John Bruer[10] has written a wonderful exposé of the myth of the first three years being critical, which should give hope to all parents and teachers who falsely believe these years are destiny. A neuroscientist deeply embedded in his profession and a well-cited author of many papers, Bruer is cautious about what neuroscience can say to parents about child reading, preferring to say 'absolutely nothing', although we would temper that with an additional word *yet*.

Take the argument that the building blocks of the brain and the development of neural connections are developed in the first three years. Yes they are, but they also change rapidly over the years. At birth we have approximately the same synaptic densities that we do as adults – but there is also rapid synapse formation, and there is much elimination beginning at puberty. Also, this growing and eliminating process does not follow the same pattern as our growth in our ability to learn: More synapses do not necessarily mean more brain power. Even further, the early growth in synapses is impervious to the quantity or stimulation, either to deprivation or to overstimulation – the early growth is more a genetic attribute of humans than an influence of the environment.

Bruer also attacks the notion that there are 'critical periods' such that if a child does not develop specific skills in these periods it is then too late to remedy this later. Most learning is 'not confined to windows of opportunities that slam shut' (p. 103). Yes, he says, we should be attentive to ensuring sensory receptors are working, be sensitive to language problems and hearing loss at the earliest possible time as these indeed can harm later skills in learning. Most of all, however, we need to care about parent–child attachment and the quality of relationships, as 'children show significantly better cognitive and language development when they are cared for by adults who engage with them in frequent affectionate responsive interactions' (p. 191). So these early years are important, just not deterministic.

Our message is to focus on the basics of learning – through the development of language, talking, skills in listening, asking 'why' questions, helping your child build a theory about their world, and beginning the fundamentals of concepts about print and a sense of ordination, patterning, and skills with numbers. Ellen Galinsky[11] has an excellent list of early literacy skills: It's about expression, it's about understanding rather than drills, and it's about enjoyment and playful ways of learning. It's about connecting the visual with the verbal, it's about concepts about print (holding the book the right way up, moving from left to right), and it's about talking, listening, discussing, and imagining. And it's about encouraging children to talk about ideas, it's about making fun to crack the code (listening to sounds, noting letters), and it's about promoting expression in all forms. She also advocates for helping children in estimating magnitudes of numbers, and we would add that rhyme is an excellent precursor of reading as it emphasizes listening to sounds.

No matter the school, you can be the leader in learning for your child at home, helping them through times with teachers who have a lesser impact on them or whom your child cannot relate to. Early missed opportunities can be regained. Home is the safe haven, the warm environment in which to explore what they do not know, as well as for testing what they think they know. It is language, language, language that matters most in the early years.

Concluding comments

The major message is to engage in talking and listening to your child, create opportunities to expand their exposure to language (e.g., reading stories, taking them on visits to explore new environments), and attend to their many queries about their world. The aim is to negate any Matthew effect and make sure all students are accelerated in their learning.

Notes

1 Hart, B., & Risley, T. R. (2003). The early catastrophe: The 30 million word gap by age 3. *American Educator, 27*(1), 4–9.

2 Pfost, M., Hattie, J., Dörfler, T., & Artelt, C. (2014). Individual differences in reading development: A review of 25 years of empirical research on Matthew effects in reading. *Review of Educational Research, 84*(2), 203–244.

3 Suskind, D., Suskind, B., & Lewinter-Suskind, L. (2015). *Thirty million words: Building a child's brain: tune in, talk more, take turns.* Dutton Books.

4 Tough, P. (2016). *Helping children succeed: What works and why.* Random House.

5 Medina, J. (2014). *Brain rules for baby, Updated and expanded: How to raise a smart and happy child from zero to five.* Pear Press.

6 Ferjan Ramírez, N., Lytle, S. R., Fish, M., & Kuhl, P. K. (2019). Parent coaching at 6 and 10 months improves language outcomes at 14 months: A randomized controlled trial. *Developmental Science, 22*(3), e12762.

7 Blaiklock, K. (2013). Talking with children when using prams while shopping. *New Zealand Research in Early Childhood Education, 16,* 15–28.

8 Zeedyk, M. S. (2008). *Promoting social interaction for individuals with communicative impairments: Making contact.* Jessica Kingsley Publishers.

9 Gilmore, A., & Hattie, J. (2000). *Evaluation of the assessment resource banks in schools: Final report.* University of Canterbury, Department of Education, Unit for Studies in Educational Evaluation, and Auckland: University of Auckland, School of Education.

10 Bruer, J. T. (1999). *The myth of the first three years: A new understanding of early brain development and lifelong learning.* Simon and Schuster.

11 Galinsky, E. (2010). *Mind in the making: The seven essential life skills every child needs.* HarperCollins.

PART

IV

The big-picture story

I appreciate that my child is not perfect, nor am I

1 Do not be a helicopter but be a responsive or open-to-learning parent

- You are not aiming for perfect children. You cannot micromanage their lives, particularly if you want them to self-regulate their learning and lives (especially when you are not there with them).

- The alternative to helicopter parenting is to become an 'open-to-learning' or responsive parent who teaches their children to listen and appreciate (though not necessarily agree with) the viewpoints of others.

- Being open to learning requires a safe context in which to have discussions, explore ideas, and hear the views of others.

2 Developing the dignity of risk

- Children need the right to take reasonable risks that help develop their positive sense of self and cope with the buzzing, sometimes booming, and often bewildering world they live and grow in. Your job is to teach them what 'reasonable' means in risk-taking.

- Developing the dignity of risk involves shared thinking, shared reactions, and shared decision-making, leading to the child learning how to process the situation, the choices, and the opportunities to react.

3 Teaching your child to say no

- Boundaries define your child and establish their sense of self or who they are (their identity). These boundaries are often loose

DOI: 10.4324/9781003257028-13

rather than rigid. Boundaries can change depending on the situation, who the child is with, and context. Learning to say 'no' helps with setting these boundaries.

- Saying 'no' helps the moral purpose of when the 'we' is more important than the 'I'.

This chapter acknowledges that as parents we are far from perfect, and therein lies opportunity. Our aim is to become 'open-to-learning' parents, be responsive to opportunities to improve, and create a high trust and safe family climate to make errors, make sense of the world, when and how to say 'no', and develop the dignity of risk.

Parents love telling stories. It's funny thinking back to the stories that my parents told and how each time they told these stories they get longer, bigger, more dangerous, and more exaggerated. One of the stories that my parents still talk about and have enhanced over the years was one from when I was 3 years old. We were staying in an apartment building on the second floor (in the latest version it is now the 15th floor). It was the second floor and there was an indoor open staircase.

As a child, I was a climber. I would get up on things, climb out of windows and onto tables. But this day was a bit different. The room we were staying in at this apartment building had a balcony. Now as a 3-year-old I have no memory of this, but for some reason, I thought it would be a good idea to climb over the railing of the balcony. There I was, 3 years old, and on the wrong side of the balcony on the second floor of the apartment building. I was very proud of myself, so I called Mum and Dad to see my accomplishment. You can imagine their reaction, or rather their thought process, because they knew if they screamed (as they wanted to) I might have had a fright and let go. They calmly walked over, grabbed me, and threw me back into the room. Now the real reactions can begin. I am lucky that I cannot remember what that was.

As parents, we all have these stories. The stories of when our children scared the living daylights out of us. It is a natural thing to worry about our kids and to want to shield them from harm. But how much can we actually protect them? This chapter is all about the love of risk-taking. Children are naturally inquisitive and want to explore the world. This is an amazing attribute to foster, but as parents we may think that risk-taking is allowing them to get into danger, when that is not it at all.

> *A child takes risks all the time. The first time they try to stand up is a risk. They have no idea what it feels like to stand, but they know they want to get up and move. So they use all the strength they have and they try to get to their feet, and what happens? They fall straight back down. This was a risk, but as parents we celebrate the effort and know that it will be okay even if they fall because we know the reward is greater than the risk. This is what we need to teach and instill in our children what is a risk and what is dangerous and to think about both and make the decision.*
>
> *As a teacher, as well as a parent, I try to instill this mind frame in the students I teach each day. They have learned that if they raise their hand and try to answer the question, they run the risk of getting the answer wrong. For some kids, they have done this and the outcome was not pleasant. They had someone laugh at them or they got embarrassed. This means that they will think twice about raising their hand again.*
>
> *Teachers work tirelessly to show that these risks can lead to learning. Mistakes are not a bad thing but a way to learn. Think back to Chapter 8 about fostering mistakes. This is the same as risk-taking. Yes, the outcome can be negative, but if we think and learn from it, then it's not all bad. But as parents, if we shield and protect our children from any negative experience this can lead to negative outcomes and poor learning strategies, and we are not raising children who see risk-taking as a positive. There is dignity in risk, as we allow our children to learn.*

1   Do not be a helicopter but be a responsive or open-to-learning parent

It did not take us long after becoming parents to stop criticizing other parents, as we learned we could not always control our own kids. They can say the darnedest things. Art Linkletter was a US personality who probably was one of the first to host a reality show. His show involved interviewing children, and the premise was that

[c]hildren under ten and women over seventy give the best interviews on the air today for the identical reason: They speak the plain unvarnished truth. They dish out in no uncertain terms, with heartfelt emotion coloring each phrase. No concealing,

faltering, hypocritical editorializing among the very young and very old! If you don't want the truth – better not ask them! And don't be shocked if it's phrased in primitive terms.

Your children are not perfect. Yes, you want to teach them appropriate behavior, respect others, and know the norms of society that you wish them to have. The dilemma is that every parent has high expectations for their children, and so they should – nearly every 4-year-old is gifted, says funny and wise things, and has perfect manners (when they want to). But they will mess up, not understand, and blurt out inappropriate comments and criticisms.

There are many descriptors of the parent who wants perfection.

- The *helicopter* parent hovers over their kids, all the time, so what chance do they have for learning how to be independent and knowing how to act and talk – their parents will make these decisions or whisk them out of the scene to land somewhere else so they can be safe and perfect.

- The *jet-fighter* parent waits more in the wings but is ready to sweep in to save their precious ones in the slightest sign of trouble or stress for the child.

- The *snowplow* or *lawnmower* parent is prepared to steamroll ahead of their child to ensure success and privilege.

- The *snowflake* parent continually claims their child is special and needs special treatment.

- The *magic bullet* parent demands the secret you have been hiding in your bottom drawer to make their child brilliant, and if they are not brilliant you are the problem.

- The *bonsai* parent wants a perfectly controlled environment and continues to tweak the environment to move the child even more towards perfection, making the child look good to others, and monitoring the child's external presentation skills.

- The *gifted* parent continually claims that their child is gifted, needs a gifted program, should mix only with other gifted children, and should not be sullied or slowed down by the dummies.

- The *social media* parent does not seem to care if the teacher has a life and bombards the teacher with questions, reactions, and opinions (not always mentioning their precious one but the messages are clearly about them).

- The *expert* parent teacher knows how to teach better than the teacher.

- The *drama* parents who can so successfully blow up a minor school incident into World War III (with tears, yelling, and demanding justice from the top down).

All these helicopter-type parents aim to have children like them, exhibiting the same senses of privilege. If you micromanage your child, chances are they will try to micromanage others, which is not how classrooms or society works. If you are a parent who is demanding or anxious to be 'right', expects to be saved by others, less likely to take responsibility for your actions, or lack confidence and run for miles from challenging situations – so will your child.

The alternative to being this sort of parent is to become an 'open-to-learning' or responsive parent.

Viviane Robinson[1] has developed the concept of open-to-learning conversations for school leaders, and her messages resonate loudly with parents as well. For parents, open-to-learning conversations are relevant when they are learning how their children are thinking and their children are learning how the parents are thinking. This is particularly so when parents and children work together toward decisions and judgments, are answering questions of why and why not, and discussing what to then do, think, and enact. Being open to learning means parents respect their children by listening and aiming to understand their children's thinking and decision-making. The opposite is 'closed to learning', which is expressed as edicts such as 'Do as you are told', and where there is no opportunity to hear the child's thinking. This does not mean parents do not have rights or power or that children have highly developed reasoning and thinking skills – they often don't: What distinguishes the two (being open or closed to learning) is not what the conversation is about but whether there is openness to learning about the validity of one's point of view.

Such openness to learning is built on, feeds on, and generates high trust, which can be the most valuable attribute to have in difficult situations when your child most needs you. Parents build this trust so they can deal with tricky and difficult issues. You do need to show your child how to listen to others' views, listen to their own views, and learn how they and others can challenge their views. They also should know how to invite alternative views, give and receive feedback, and deal with conflict. When parents, or their children, impose their views, there are often negative emotional reactions, winners and losers, and loss of the trust which is so needed for the hard times.

Viviane Robinson has a long list of recommended strategies for increasing school leader responsiveness, and these are just as applicable to parents. They include talking about your reasoning, listening to your child's reasoning (remembering it's not a contest, or about right or wrong, but showing respect by listening), and treating your views as hypotheses, not truths. Look for evidence you may be wrong, and listen deeply, especially when your child (or partner) may have different views from yours. Expect high standards and constantly check how you are helping your child reach these standards, and ensure high levels of turn taking because lectures rarely have lasting effects. Work hard to identify the right problem in any discussion and share the problem before you give any answers. Finally, check the impact of your parenting to see the quality of your decisions and actions.

The payoff from being an open-to-learning parent comes in times of conflict, whenever there are differences in views or performance is unsatisfactory. The trust you have built and the sense that it is normal for your family to identify and discuss problems makes it much easier to seek alternative views and provides a safe environment for your child to think aloud. Your child may not agree with your decision or actions (you are still the parent), but responsiveness creates a model for your child to also become responsive to you and others.

Some of the phrases you might want in your 'responsive' toolbox (again from Viviane Robinson) include

- I need to tell you about a possible concern I have about . . .
- I think we may have different views . . .
- I realize this may not be how you see it . . .
- I'm disappointed in your behavior because . . .
- I want to work with you to address their concerns . . .
- What do you think?
- You haven't said much so far. . . . Do you see it differently?
- This time I really want to understand more about your situation . . .
- What other possibilities are there?
- We both agree this is unacceptable as it is . . .
- It sounds like we see the problem the same way . . .

Do not confuse responsiveness and being open to learning as defaulting on your decision-making role as parents. You are still 'responsible' for raising your kids, and sometimes they do not see through the consequences of their actions, sometimes they need to be taught more optimal ways of behaving and thinking, and sometimes they do make mistakes. Responsiveness creates a context in which you can have discussions and teach your children while maintaining great relations, high levels of trust, and respect for you as a parent. These are the perfect assets for your children when they are making and dealing with friends, and dealing with other people, particularly in tricky situations. Having these skills pays off particularly during the adolescent years.

Your job is NOT to create the road for your child to walk down or to sweep the road clear so they have an untrammeled pathway but to be behind them as walk down the roads and help them develop coping strategies for dealing with the many turns, cul-de-sacs, and highways they will confront. Families are not like a bus service, where everyone gets on, is driven on the same route down the road, and is dropped off safely at the end of each day. Instead, we want to raise Uber drivers – each child may start from a different place, drive a different route, and end at a different end point. But you want them to be safe, make wise choices, and decide on worthwhile destinations. You do the latter not by clearing the road for them but by teaching them the skills to navigate the road themselves.

2 Developing the dignity of risk

There is a dignity of risk that parents need to teach their children. This means that your children have the rights to take reasonable risks that can be important to developing their positive sense of self and cope with the world they live and grow in. This does not mean taking crazy risks, extreme risks, or ridiculous risks but rather learning what a 'reasonable' risk is, have coping strategies to deal with the consequences of taking these risks, and knowing when and when not to take a risk. The dignity of risk needs to be taught before adolescence, as this is the phase where they are expected to be away from you, be in situations where risk is ever-present, and when daring to take risks in front of friends is all the more important to them (see Chapter 5 on reputation enhancement).

Think of your own life – you took risks (having kids was one), you fell over, you went down blind alleys, suffered, made mistakes, upset some people – but you got there. You learned skills of resilience, how to reframe negatives to learn from them and move forward, and, yes, sometimes you succeeded and sometimes not. It is the skills of risk-taking that parents need to teach their children. This is not teaching them to rush in blindly or continue down roads that are unlikely to yield value but enabling them to know how to weigh the options of risk. No matter how much you would like to keep them in cotton wool, the world out there – the schools they attend, the neighborhood they live in, the friends and others they meet – is not always safe, secure, and predictable.

The notion of 'dignity of risk' was developed by Robert Perske[2] when he noted the indignity of overprotection of many people with intellectual disabilities, and the concept has now been applied to many situations (physical illness, dementia). We apply it here to parenting. Perske noted that risk is NOT necessarily a precursor to harm or negative outcomes. Nor was he talking about overestimating or denying risk, but developing the autonomy skills to live in an often unpredictable world. Denying risk denies autonomy, impacts negatively on how children will act and react in risky situations, and restricts the choices that they consider in weighing how to cope with risk.

Once again, developing the dignity of risk involves shared thinking, shared reactions, and shared decision-making, all leading to the child learning how to process the situation and decide how to react. Allowing the dignity of risk means respecting their consideration of these issues and decisions by listening to them 'think aloud' about the risks and how they intend to minimize harm. It involves teaching them about other options, making sure they do not go down the wrong roads, and ensuring they have a graceful fallback when things do not work out.

An associated notion to the dignity of risk is the dignity of relationships, a concept our co-author of *Distance Learning Playbook for Parents*[3] Rosalind Wiseman has promoted.[4] She argues that dignity is given and respect is earned, and a denial of dignity for your children (or they of you) is often the root of the conflict. She outlines ten elements. We have placed 'your child' into the sentences.

1 Validate your child for their talents, hard work, thoughtfulness, and help.
2 Acknowledge your child by giving them full attention by listening, validating, and responding.

3 Allow your child the benefit of the doubt assumes that they have good motives and are acting with integrity.

4 Develop feelings of inclusion, which means making your child feel that they belong at all levels of relationships.

5 Provide safety so that your child is free of harm, shame, or humiliation and feels free to speak without fear of retribution.

6 Understand your child by giving them a chance to explain their perspective and listening so we're prepared to be changed by what we hear.

7 Approach your child as neither inferior nor superior, giving them the freedom to express themselves without fear of being judged.

8 Encourage fairness by treating your child justly, with quality and equity.

9 Foster independence by empowering your child to act on their own behalf so that they learn to feel in control of their lives and experience a sense of hope and possibility.

10 Ensure accountability by taking inviting your child to take responsibility for their actions.

These ten elements entail not taking the bait but showing your child how to act with restraint, not denying what you have done to protect your pride and power, and being prepared to say sorry genuinely when you make a mistake. It involves showing that dignity comes from within and doesn't depend on others alone for validation of one's worth, involves not allowing one's need for connection to outweigh one's dignity, and involves knowing that you matter and your experiences and feelings are important. Other aspects are being open to hearing how others interpret your actions, being open to and receiving feedback and criticism, realizing blaming and shaming others fixes nothing, and that to create intimacy with others it is important to speak the truth not the gossip.

3 Teaching your child to say no

Most 3–4-year-olds love asking 'why', and as we noted earlier this sense of wonder helps them better understand the world around them. Sadly, by age 8 they will reduce their 'why' curiosity and switch to 'what' questions as the message they get from schools (rightly or wrongly) is that the purpose of schooling is to learn lots of facts – to emulate Siri and Google. When we ask 8–10-year-olds who is the best learner in this class and why, they typically identify the student who knows much and knows the answers quickly (both are far from the attributes of good learners we are promoting throughout this book). During adolescence, they switch to 'why not' as they assert independence and want more say and control over their competing requests of their time, attention, and love.

The world out there is not always a safe place. Among the worst scenarios is other and often older children or adults leading your child astray, and this can entail goading them into keeping secrets about poor behavior and interactions. The question is how to teach your child when and how to say 'no', such that 'No means no'.

Boundaries define your child. Boundaries establish their sense of self or identity – who they are – and these boundaries are often loose rather than rigid and can change depending on the situation, who you are with, and context. In particular, adolescents may need reminding of the need for space boundaries as they can make poor decisions about personal space. Teaching them these boundaries is a key task of parents. It is the same for you as parents – yes your child (initially) may expect you to be perfect, a saint, and a most learned parent. But they will find us out, although that does not mean we are the opposite. Having boundaries does not mean you never take risks or make bad decisions; boundaries allow you and your children to cope with imperfections. Your children are also expected to be sons or daughters, siblings, students, friends, and many other roles – and it is a big ask, especially for younger children especially when they enter new situations and meet new people to work out these boundaries.

A core skill in boundary decisions that you need to teach your children is when and how to say 'no'. Consider the contrast Gert Biesta[5] makes between Adolf Eichmann and Rosa Parks. Eichmann realized his potential; the schools in Germany at the time provided him the skills to successfully participate in their economy and society, and he certainly looked after himself in every aspect of his well-being. Rosa Parks also went to school, but because of the restrictions upon African Americans she did not have the opportunities or provisions to attain her potential. However, unlike Eichmann, she did have the courage to say 'no'. She, much more than Eichmann, contributed to developing a moral purpose contrary to the norms of her society, to appreciate the 'we' more than the 'I', and to use her power of 'no' to refuse to participate in the economy and society of the time.

We know which one contributed most wonderfully to society, to the economy, and to the well-being of society.

In some societies (e.g., Eastern Confucian-based countries) saying 'no' is to be avoided, and often it is better to avoid answering or deviate the conversation so a no or refusal is not provided. Everyone knows people who can openly and directly say no and some who equivocate and do not like to say no. For some, 'no' is not a problem, just a statement, whereas others waffle, are tentative and use 'maybe', and have difficulties with saying no in case it indicates a lack of gratitude or is a mark of disrespect. Then there are those who follow up, requesting or demanding reasons for someone saying no. There are also skills to recognize the context when a direct 'no' is more or less acceptable. Your child has to work out if the stimulus leading to their saying no is a demand, a request, an invitation, an offer, a rejection, or a suggestion.

When children are in a situation in which saying 'no' is an option, you need to work out whether they are saying it for protection, to maintain identity, for defiance, or because of uncertainty. You may need to know when to follow up by asking for their reasons why saying 'no'. The message you want to model is when it is appropriate for them to insist that 'no means no'. Our nonverbals in these situations can be great cues as to the nature of the 'no' response. The more eye contact (by you to the child, and from the child to you), then usually the more certain you are about the follow-up to the 'no' – for example, eye contact could indicate that no is not an option or could communicate that 'I will accept reasons for your no, let's look at alternatives'. They will experience peer pressure to engage in tasks that are not acceptable, and teaching them to repeat 'no' is important to show they will stand firm in that decision. You also need to teach them how to say 'no' without it being a rejection of that person.

If you force, threaten, belittle, shame, or punish your child every time they say no, they will hardly learn to do otherwise with others, and they will treat 'no' from others as requiring these reactions – thus more likely leading to rejection. Hence, there is a skill when a 'no' is enforced, or when reasoning is invited (maybe then leading still to the no). This skill can involve the use of phrasing, tone, and body language (which is why some kids have more trouble when they say no on social media as the nature of the 'no' can be harder to interpret (is it a real no; is it asking for reasoning, for options, or is it rejection?).

Pick the times to celebrate your child's 'no' response, and realize that they need to learn this skill of accepting no from others – which goes to the heart of their skill to stand in the shoes of others and understand the implications of the no. This is tough for young children (under 5) to do and thus why it is important to understand the limits of how younger children can react to a 'no'. However, sometimes overexplaining is not worth it, not welcomed, not heard, and not appropriate. At these moments, you are the parent, not the friend, and do not say (as one of us did to the other), 'You look ugly when you are angry'. Sometimes you can reframe the request so that 'yes' becomes an option, or you can redirect unwelcome behaviors (rather than saying, 'Stop screaming', say, 'Let me hear your whisper voice'), or you can give alternatives ('Would you prefer to whisper or tell me what you want me to hear later?'). There is a power in 'no'.

Concluding comments

Perfection is not the goal. Let your children make mistakes as see these mistakes as opportunities for learning. The parent's role is to be open to learning opportunities, create high levels of trust and safety to make and learn from mistakes, and teach your child what reasonable means in risk-taking and how to say and react to 'no'. The boundaries between risk and safety and between yes and no are too often fuzzy and not strong demarcations. How we deal with these boundaries defines us and how we teach our children to identify, react, and live with their responses at the boundaries goes to the heart of developing the child's moral purpose.

Notes

1 Robinson, V. (2009). *Open-to-learning conversations: Background paper.* Module 3: Building Trust in Schools Through Open-to-learning Conversations. First-time Principals Programme.
2 Perske, R. (1972). The dignity of risk and the MR. *Mental Retardation, 10*(1), 24.
3 Fisher, D., Frey, N., Almarode, J., Hattie, J., & Wiseman, R. (2021). *The distance learning playbook for parents: Teaching for engagement and impact in any setting.* Corwin Press.
4 https://culturesofdignity.com/risk-factor-the-truth-about-dares/
5 Biesta, G. (2020). Can the prevailing description of educational reality be considered complete? On the Parks-Eichmann paradox, spooky action at a distance and a missing dimension in the theory of education. *Policy Futures in Education, 18*(8), 1011–1025.

10

I am an evaluator of my impact

1 It's about impact

- Every time you interact with your child, if you say, 'My job today is to evaluate my impact on my children', then great things are more likely to happen.

- Impact relates to turning your children on to your passions and seeing something more in them than they may see in themselves.

- Parenting for impact entails great diagnosis about where your child begins in a learning task, choosing and implementing interventions that have a high probability of success, and finally evaluating the impact of your intervention.

2 You know more than you think you do

- You do not want to know 'what works' but 'what works best'.

- Parents need to see the effects of their words, actions, encouragement, and expectations through the eyes of their children.

- The mark of an empowered person in Western society is a person who knows what to do when they do not know what to do.

3 There is no one right way

- Given that parenting is so different around the world, there is clearly no one right way to raise children.

This chapter invites a laser focus on the impact we have as parents. The key guiding questions in parenting are 'evaluating our impact on our children', making the adjustments, smelling the roses when successful, and understanding when and why our impact may not be as we intended. To become parents, we have had so many opportunities to develop the skills of evaluating our impact – so when

DOI: 10.4324/9781003257028-14

135

becoming parents, the focus of this impact turns to our influence on our children. We know more than we think we do – and across the world, there are so many different ways of parenting, but the common denominator is to positively impact the learning lives of our children.

1 It's about impact

We've left the most important mind frame till last, and indeed the other nine mind frames are subsets of this mind frame. Every time you interact with your child, if you say, 'My job today is to evaluate my impact on my children', then great things are more likely to happen. When parents enter the contract to have children (accidentally or not) they take on the role of impact-extraordinaire. Just as parents' views about their children may change as the children (and parents) grow, the nature of impact that parents would like to have, do have, and could have also changes.

Impact is a powerful word. The question is did your efforts to ensure that your child learned something actually result in learning. It is less a focus on parenting and more a focus on the impact of your parenting. Parents need to ask: 'Was there an impact on my child's learning and behavior?' Too much attention is spent on the processes of how to parent and not enough is spent on the outcomes of the parenting.

For example, when parents talk to their children about school-work and focus only on grades and not on learning, this can lead to a negative impact. Yes, you want children to earn good grades. But those grades should reflect learning and not compliance. Imagine what it must feel like and what powerful messages are conveyed when parents continually reinforce high grades or when they ask their child who is the brightest in the class. By age 8, most kids know where they fit in the hierarchy of the class achievement lists and sadly continually receive messages about their rightful place in this league table – surely the role of parents and teachers is to disrupt this expectation and find ways to help students raise their expectations – and then realize them. Never say your job is to help your children reach their potential – your job is to help them exceed what they think is their potential.

We have asked thousands of people around the world about the teachers who have had a major positive impact on them. When we ask an audience to put up their hand if they can recall zero, one, two, three, or more such teachers, the usual answer is two (out of about 50 teachers they would have experienced). In many ways, your parent role is to support your child learning through the other 48 teachers, and hope you do not meet a horrid teacher who can damage your child. A bad teacher one year doubles the chance of your child being turned off school; over two years, this almost guarantees it. This is not to say there are no good teachers among the 48, but rather, they are not exceptional.

Now to why those two teachers were so positively impactful on you.

We had access to 658 adults who responded to a national request (led by the prime minister) asking people to nominate the best teacher and why.[1] An analysis of the keywords found the most common words were motivation and encouragement (14%), personable (11%), guidance and mentoring (11%), opened a career path (10%), inspiring (8%), enhanced learning (7%), and increased love of learning (4%; see Figure 10.1 for a Wordle of the major responses). These words and claims were grouped into three higher order themes: the teacher was influential (53%), inspired (34%), and passionate (12%). The typical influential teacher increased confidence, was engaging, enhanced the learning experience and love of learning, provided guidance and mentoring, and opened career paths – all these led to the often-cited claim that the teacher saw something in the person as a child that the person did not see in themselves. The inspiring

FIGURE 10.1 A word cloud based on the 1,203 coded responses

teachers were amazing, encouraging, inspiring, patient, personable, and supportive. The passionate teacher was dedicated, determined, enthusiastic, passionate, and committed. These three dimensions were similar across socioeconomic zones of the schools, the size of the school, whether schools were elementary or high schools, and across curriculum areas. Indeed, there were almost no references to particular curriculum areas or to teachers who taught specific content to these respondents: The relationships, the expectations, and the passion were more critical than the particular curriculum.

John can recall Ms Fisher, his teacher when he started school at 5; Mr Andrews, his high school English teacher who started the year stating that his job was not getting the class through the exams but turning them on to English (he did both); but most of all he remembers Mr Tomlinson, his final high school year teacher of mathematics. Here is a letter he sent to Mr Tomlinson in 2010.

Mr. Tomlinson

(Thanks for the invite to call you by your first name, but old habits don't fade that quickly.)

It was a pleasure to get your letter – I am sure I was one of the many who has passed through your class and with your incredible memory for names, one question we asked (way back then) was whether there was a fade factor to make room for the next year's cohort. Obviously from your letter not!

High school was not among my most treasured memories. Many aspects do not bring back great memories, but there were highlights. It was wonderful, in retrospect, that we had a limited number of options – and making us stay in mathematics was one. I was ok, and probably, if I had a choice, I would have stopped doing it after SC. It was in your class that it suddenly came together. That was the moment when all that rote learning began to make sense. In particular, I recall that it was fun to work out angles in geometry questions, in calculus you enabled me to see movement and space, and algebra was always a favorite. It was your proficiency to make it all make sense and have fun doing it. You spared us no secrets about the amount of work we would have to do to master the level required, but your passionate love of your subject and enjoyment when we dummies got it. It was a no penalty class provided you put in the effort and listened. I then went to Dunedin Teachers College and the University of Otago and picked up statistics – which I then went to include right through to PhD level. Your influence.

I intend this year to be a great year. Janet and I have been married 25 years, I have been a full professor for 25 years, and last week turned 60 (wow, you were indeed a young teacher when at TBHS). As a professor of education I am often asked about excellent teachers. I use a story – name (actually name in your mind) the teachers that had a positive influence on you during your school years? I then ask you to put your hand up if you can think of zero, one, two, three, four, or more. The modal number is always two! Wow. And we have about 50 teachers in primary and secondary, so about four qualify. Then for the reasons – the key is 'they make us love their passion for their subject and they saw something in us we did not see in ourselves'. You have always been my litmus test – and my number one in this exercise. And I now thank you for this. There are many gatekeepers in our lives and in your case you were the one who opened these gates for me.

In 1973, I returned home to Timaru looking for a 9-month job before I went to Toronto. I was at the local store when Mr. Walsh, the headmaster, walked in and asked what I was doing in Timaru (living over the road meant he 'knew' me, and my sister was a friend of his daughters). Well, he said, Mr. Manning had a heart attack last night and I need a teacher till he returns, you start on Monday!. I must confess Mr. Manning and I were never on the same planet – and among the most horrific teachers I experienced, sarcastic, no learning (music consisted of putting a record on and making us listen for 40 minutes and refusing to tell us the composer as we were too dumb to know – and I do recall someone (you) telling us about some music you heard drifting across – Duff's Ding Dongs.

What irony to be teaching his classes. And thoroughly enjoyed it. It was the time that caning was banned – what a staff meeting that was – the end of teaching as they knew it for some. Bertie the Biff was retired, and a new wave slowly moved across the school.

During the writing of my recent book on Visible Learning, I kept coming back to passion and high expectations. Yes, I am a psychometrician, and evidence based, quantitative etc., and many seem surprised that I advocate more research on passion.

The Timaru Old Boys have honored me with the Teschamaker Cup – it requires a trip to Timaru so this time I would like to meet up.

Till then
Best wishes
John

We invite you to locate your influential, passionate, and inspired teachers and write to them about their impact. This is what teachers live for – to have an impact on students – so it would be so valuable and powerful for them to hear your story.

The same message as to what makes teachers a positive and memorable influence applies equally to parents; impact relates to turning your children on to your passions, and seeing something more in them they see in themselves.

It raises the moral purpose questions about what all caregivers mean by *impact* and whether and how your children experience this impact. This mind frame requires that you shift your thinking from whether your child is compliant to the ways in which the tasks you ask of your child have impacted their learning. It also invokes the notion of 'backward design' – starting from what you desire as the end point and working backward. It requires communicating to your child up front about what the criterion of success looks like, identifying where the child is now relative to these notions of success, and then working with your child to move them from the now to the desired success. It is a lot like how video games are structured (see Chapter 8). It is less about doing the task, and more about the success of the outcomes.

In schools, we call this the DIIE model as in 'Teachers are to DIIE for':[2] Diagnosis (or Discovery) of what your child can and cannot do now, Intervention or the desired ways you want to teach your child how to accomplish the task, Implementation of the intervention, and Evaluation or simply using the same methods you used for early diagnoses repeated at the end. Parents are to DIIE for too.

Diagnosis	Understanding what your child brings to the task, their motivations, and their willingness to engage.
Intervention	Having multiple interventions such that if one does not work with your child, you can change to another intervention.
Implementation	Making sure your intervention is implemented with fidelity and quality.
Evaluation	Checking to see if the implementation of your intervention moved your child's learning from the starting point to success.

2 You know more than you think you do

Dr Spock, the famous pediatrician from the 1940s who influenced John's parents, argued that parents do know more than they think and that certainly there is no one right way of being a parent. Different societies and cultures have very different notions of what it means to be a good person, what it means to raise children, and what it means to be successful. A quick review of parenting across cultures shows simply there is no right way – a lot depends on what you want your child to do when a child and when they become a teenager and young adult.

We make this critical distinction between 'when a child and when they become when a teenager and young adult' to make clear that childhood is 'the now' for the child, and life at these ages are not always for preparation as an adult. You cannot predict the future, you will not know the range and nature of many jobs and careers 20 years hence, and you will miss the joy and pains of seeing your child as a real person from the moment they are born. But we do and should worry about what we want our child to be when they are teens and beyond.

For us, the outcomes relate to a person having a sense of competence, being able to respect self and respect others, and having a degree of autonomy to act and be responsible for one's actions. Such self-determination is a major outcome in Western society and much of what is written in this book aims for these attributes in the 'now' (while the child is still a child) and in preparation for later when they are indeed meant to be more autonomous in determining their actions, reactions, and futures. If you want your child to be a criminal (not respect others), a clone of yourself (not autonomous), or incapable of thinking through the consequences of their actions (not competent), this book is not for you.

In preparing for writing this book, we (John and Kyle) investigated the evidence about the influence of the home and parenting on children's learning (see the Appendix). Our conclusions were similar to the Visible Learning research based on achievement in schools. In this school-related Visible Learning work, we used more than 100,000 studies based on over a third of a billion students, and the most fascinating finding is that 'almost everything we do to a child increases their learning'. 'Alright', you say, 'so I can shut the book and do what I want'. No. The message is the opposite – be wary of people telling you, 'This worked for me', or 'Here's what works'. They will be right – almost everything does work but only to a small degree – as the evidence shows, while 'anything' may work a bit, it doesn't work well or achieve significant change or promote great learning. It's not about whether there's an effect but rather about the size of the effect.

The major implication for schools is that teachers should not set the bar so low by asking, 'What works to increase learning?' but should raise the bar by asking 'What works *best* to increase learning?' It is the same for parenting, you do not want to know merely 'what works' but rather 'what works best'.

We also discovered that those above-average effects in school-related learning had little to do with the structural influences (class size, ability grouping), the nature of the school (charter, private, public), the nature of the curriculum, or the presence or nature of tests. What was important for nearly all the above-average effects was 'how teachers think'. It is the nature of the moment-by-moment judgments that teachers make about what to do next considering what the child can already do or not do that matters. This is 'evaluative thinking'.

Our Visible Learning mantra for teachers is that teachers should see learning through the eyes of students, and students should become their own teachers. Similarly, with parenting, the mantra is that parents need to see the effects of their words, actions, encouragement, and expectations through the eyes of their children. If you want to be a better parent, learn to see what you look like, feel like, and do by imagining you are the child. Your aim is to help your child become the teacher so that when they have to make decisions (especially when you are not present) they can see their actions as others would, know how their actions impact others around them, and know what best to do next.

The mark of an empowered person in our Western society is a person who knows what to do when they do not know what to do. This requires a high sense of competence, a great awareness of relating to others, and a sense of autonomy that relates to owning the decisions you choose to make. Teach your child to know what to do when they do not know what to do – that is, how to seek help, how to ask questions, how to find information, how to navigate between multiple options, how to evaluate the worthwhileness of information, and how to see the world through others' eyes.

3 There is no one right way

The differences in the experiences of parenting are enormous – in your neighborhood, in your country, across many countries, and generations. There is a great deal to learn from these different approaches to parenting. In Bali, for example, babies are not meant to touch the ground until they are 3 months old, and the name of the child is a function of their birth order (Wayan, then Made, Nyoman, and Ketut). In Greece and Mauritania, parents spit at the baby three times to ward off evil spirits. In Ireland, the bad spirits are banished by crumbling part of the top tier of the wedding cake on the baby. In India, there is a festival where babies are tossed about 15 meters from the parents into a sheet held by friends (do not try that at home). While Westerners emphasize face-to-face interaction with their babies, many in Africa emphasize skin-to-skin. In Kenya, parents do not make eye contact with newborns and consider talking to a baby a silly notion – their children talk without looking at them so why bother! In China, there are seven Confucian virtues that parents like to instill in their children from very early days: sincerity, diligence, endurance of hardship, perseverance, concentration, respect for teachers, and humility.[3]

Given that parenting is so different around the world, there is clearly no one right way to raise children. This would give some credibility to some experts who say the role of parents is overplayed. Given that there are so many different ways to parent, why is there almost a modern-day cultural and biological imperative to over-parent and learn the 'right way'? These days it's almost seen as neglectful to not to have your children enrolled in four different sports, many cultural activities, ensure they are angels at school, and honor them as mini-adults.

We know from research that the modern tendency to over-parent can lead children to have an overinflated sense of entitlement and that children get frustrated when they can't work themselves through a situation. There can be an even stronger tendency to further intensify parenting, as we try to prevent children from taking risks and as we pour in unprecedented levels of time with our children.

One consequence of this is that we unreasonably expect our children to return this investment with brilliance, success, and independence. When they don't, then as parents we can get very frustrated and anxious about what to do next or what went wrong. But the message is – don't be. Robert and Sarah LeVine say:

> Once American parents free themselves from the expert warnings that any deviations from current American practices will constitute trauma, abuse, or adversity for their children's development – warnings that we have shown are largely groundless – then it will be possible to learn from other cultures and reduce parental burdens to a more sensible level.
>
> (LeVine & LeVine, 2016, p. 191)

There is no one right way to parent. Parenting is 'interactive' and learned on the job – it is not a precise science. What worked today might not work tomorrow, let alone expecting what you did with one child will have the same effect on the next child. Your approach to parenting will of course be strongly influenced by the individual personality of your children. The differences between our children are huge. Parents are often left wondering how their children could have experienced the same parental influences and yet still be so different.

Parenting a child is complex and rewarding, and involves a life-changing relationship for both parents and children. The way that the unique quirks, personalities, and beliefs of each child interact with each other and with their parents will lead to quite different outcomes. Throw in the influence of siblings, other adults, friends, school, genetics, and you can see why very little about parenting is predictable.

Concluding comments

Perfection is not the goal. Let your children make mistakes and see these mistakes as opportunities for learning. The parent's role is to be open to learning opportunities, create high levels of trust and safety to make and learn from mistakes, and teach your child what reasonable means in risk-taking and how to say and react to 'no'. The boundaries between risk and safety and between yes and no are too often fuzzy and not strong demarcations. How we deal with these boundaries defines us and how we teach our children to identify, react, and live with their responses at the boundaries goes to the heart of developing the child's moral purpose.

The powerful message from the evidence is that positive parenting relates more to HOW YOU THINK than to the nature and structure of your family, your family resources, and what you do. And for positive parenting, this thinking needs to be what we call evaluative thinking. For parents, evaluative thinking is about how they see the impact of their actions on their children. It is communicating high expectations, thinking about failure and errors as opportunities to learn, demonstrating they can see their child's learning and experiences through the child's eyes, and working to teach the child how to be their own teacher.

High impact parenting for learning involves demonstrating upfront to your children what success in an activity looks like, and ensuring you set the bar for success at a level that is not too hard, not too easy, and not too boring. High impact parenting is teaching your children how to seek and receive feedback, while you demonstrably do the same. It is showing your children how to engage in deliberate practice, and learning from making mistakes – that is the core to learning.

Notes

1 Clinton, J. M., Hattie, J. A. C., & Nawab, D. (2018). The good teacher: Our best teachers are inspired, influential and passionate. In M. Harring (Ed.), *Handbook for school pedagogics* (pp. 880–888). Waxmann.

2 Hattie, J. A. C., Bustamante, V., Almarode, J., Fisher, D., & Frey, N. (2021). *Great teaching by design: From intention to implementation in the Visible Learning Classroom.* Corwin Press.

3 LeVine, R. A., & LeVine, S. (2016). *Do parents matter?: Why Japanese babies sleep soundly, Mexican siblings don't fight, and American families should just relax.* Public Affairs.

Glossary

Attachment Where we seek proximity to and emotional contact with a specific figure and to do so in certain situations, notably when frightened, anxious, tired, or ill.

Authoritarian parenting Parents who engage in 'I am right, you are the child', see the child as not able to make good decisions, and engage in verbal hostility and sometimes corporal punishment.

Authoritative (reasoning and listening) parenting Parents who create warmth and involvement, engage in appropriate reasoning and listening to the child, and create a climate of trust and fairness. We describe this form of parenting as the listening and reasonable parent, or open-to-learning parent

Big Five personality attributes A widely accepted set of five of the most critical personality attributes: extraversion (the level of sociability and enthusiasm), agreeableness (the level of friendliness and kindness), conscientiousness (the level of organization and work ethic), emotional stability (the level of calmness and tranquility), and openness to experiences (the level of creativity and curiosity).

Dignity of relationships The right to relate to others, including validating your and your child's talents and hard work, actively listening, feel included and belong, welcoming others' perspectives, encouraging fairness and autonomy, and ensuring responsibility for their thoughts and actions.

Dignity of risk The right to take reasonable risks that can be important to developing your child's positive sense of self and cope with the world they live and grow in. This does not mean taking crazy risks, extreme risks, or ridiculous risks but rather learning what a 'reasonable' risk is, having coping strategies to deal with the consequences of taking these risks, and knowing.

DIIE model A model of implementation, involving diagnosis or discovery, choosing optimal interventions, ensuring fidelity and quality of implementation, and evaluating the impact of the intervention. DIIE = diagnosis, intervention, implementation, and evaluation.

Emotion-focused coping Strategies directed at minimizing distress triggered by stressors such as anger, denial, wishful thinking, or attempts to escape stressful situations.

Evaluative thinking The core evaluative thinking skills are critical thinking, reasoning, and understanding others (how they think, reason, judge, interact) that are used to form a judgment about merit, worth, or significance. Evaluative thinking involves invoking reasoning and critical thinking in valuing evidence, leading to 'where to next' recommendations, and understanding others' points of view, leading to judgments of value or worth.

Executive functioning Relates to 'how' we think, or how we process information. There are three major components of executive functioning – inhibition, task shifting, and monitoring and updating.

Extrinsic motivation The act of doing something because we want to earn a reward or avoid punishment.

Goldilocks principle The level of difficulty in any request or task should not be too hard, not too easy, and not too boring.

Grit A passion and sustained persistence applied toward long-term achievement, with no particular concern for rewards or recognition along the way. It combines resilience, ambition, and self-control in the pursuit of goals that take months, years, or even decades.

Growth and fixed mindsets A growth mindset means you believe your intelligence and skills can be developed over time, whereas a fixed mindset believes that whatever intelligence and skills you have now are unlikely to improve (e.g., I can do it or I can't do it yet vs. I can't do it or I am open to learning it).

Inhibition The ability to concentrate on the task at hand and avoid being distracted.

Inhibition The ability to deliberately inhibit dominant, automatic, or common responses when necessary.

Intrinsic motivation The act of doing something without any obvious external rewards. You engage in the activity because it is fun, rewarding in its own right, is interesting, and there is no outside incentive or pressure to do it, such as a reward or deadline.

Matthew effect Coined from a verse in the New Testament (Matthew 25:29) which is commonly paraphrased as 'the rich get richer and the poor get poorer'.

Meta-analyses A meta-analyst collects as many articles as possible on a particular topic (e.g., by searching Google Scholar), codes them for interesting features (e.g., country of study, grade of class, ability of student), and then relates these features to an outcome (e.g., enhanced achievement, social or emotional well-being). It is a statistical method of synthesizing many studies.

Mind frame A mind frame is a way of thinking, a set of beliefs, skills, and feelings that guide talk, actions, and decisions.

Monitoring and updating Relate to the ability to manipulate the contents being held by working memory.

Need for autonomy Part of the self-determination theory, autonomy is met when the child feels that their actions are their own.

Need for competence Part of the self-determination theory, competence is met the child feels the task before them is within their skill set, and they have some control or predictability over their environment.

Need for relatedness Part of the self-determination theory, relatedness is met when a child is attached and accepted by a community, group, or family.

Open-to-learning conversations Being open to the quality of your and others' thinking, particularly when making judgments about others' thinking, actions, and reactions. It entails developing high levels of trust, paying attention to the values and motivations, and being a good listener.

Permissive parenting Parents who allow much leeway to the child, allow them free rein, and ignore a lot of misbehavior.

Problem-focused coping Strategies directed at the stressor itself: taking steps to remove or to evade it or to diminish its impact if it cannot be evaded.

Reputation enhancement Where you aim to enhance your reputation relating to skills and beliefs about yourself among your peers.

Self-determination This theory includes autonomy, relatedness, and competence. These three components work together to form our sense as a person and underlie human motivation and sense of success.

Self-regulation The capability to learn, to ask questions, invest in learning, and make mistakes without the fear of being seen as 'dumb'.

Self-regulation The processes involved in when we decide what to think, feel, say, or do. We make decisions relative to our beliefs of what is desirable behavior, our motivations to meet these standards, how we monitor situations and thoughts, and our strength to move to desired outcomes. We invoke self-monitoring (we notice and evaluate our behavior and actions), self-evaluation (making a judgment about self-monitoring information), and self-reinforcing (rewarding or attributing success towards our goals).

Shifting Also termed cognitive flexibility or task switching, the ability to move back and forth between multiple different tasks.

Task shifting The ability to shift between different tasks or across ideas.

Theory of mind One's theory of mind relates not only to our interpretation of the world and how we make sense of it but also to how we react, think, and process information about our beliefs about our world

Visible Learning Covers the research and interpretations of the synthesis of (now) over 1,700 meta-analyses relating various influences to advancing achievement in school (see https://us.corwin.com/en-us/nam/visible-learning).

Zone of proximal development Developed by Lev Vygotsky, this zone includes all the ideas, activities, and skills a child is ready to learn next – with the help of an expert.

Appendix

There is evidence about high-impact parenting

Research means 're-searching' other people's stories of their experiences or their interpretation of others' experiences. The key here is less the evidence and more the interpretation of this evidence. Our role has been to interpret this evidence in a convincing and compelling manner for you. If you do not want to know the details, it is okay to skip this Appendix and refer to it only if you want the source of the evidence for our claims and interpretations in the various chapters.

Over the past 20 years, we have embarked on a major synthesis of the meta-analysis research on learning which we have called Visible Learning. We start with an outline of this work because it has major messages for parents.

The Visible Learning story

Schools are full of dedicated teachers. Most entered the profession because they wanted to have an impact on student learning, and nearly all do. But what we found strange was that almost every teacher and school leader we met could tell us how best to teach children, and nearly all claimed to have evidence that their teaching had a positive impact on students. But how come when we were students it was not like this? We had some teachers we did not like and they did not seem to like us. Yes, some were great. But most of them were just okay.

This led to a 20-year adventure – finding the effects of as many influences on student learning as we could find. Now we have evidence from about a third of a billion students, over 100,000 studies, and over 300 influences. The most surprising finding was that almost every influence will increase children's learning. There are some negative influences — bullying, holding kids back, and repeating a year of school . . . but more than 95% of the influences on children's learning will increase their learning — on average.

These last two words — on average — are critical, as there can be wide variation in the effect of the influences on individual students. Care is always needed to seek evidence that anything done to improve learning does have a positive, above-average impact on the individual, hence the Visible Learning mantra 'Know thy impact'.

Most influences identified in our synthesis of the research are related to what is done in schools. Figure 1 shows the distribution of all the influences — the focus of interest is understanding how those influences with an above average effect are substantively different from those below the average. Working out this story is why it took close to 20 years to write the *Visible Learning* book.

An effect size is a standardized measure of impact, based on teacher assessments, standardized tests, and so on. The measure may compare two conditions (e.g., introducing a teaching method and comparing results with regular teaching) or taken over time (students complete a pretest, a new teaching intervention is applied, and a post-intervention test measures any change). In the synthesis, it is imperative to see if the average effect is applicable in all conditions or whether there are critical moderators such as ability — for example, whether the effect is similar for gifted children compared to non-gifted, similar for 5-year-olds compared to 15-years-olds, similar in the US compared to China compared to Australia, similar for males and females, similar for upper and lower socioeconomic background schools, and much more.

We were not only surprised to find little evidence that effect sizes varied according to the moderators but also excited because it meant we could generalize about what works best for learning, regardless of moderators such as ability or socioeconomic background.

Table 1 provides a list of some of the influences and their effect. An average effect has an effect size of 0.4, so anything above this score is an above-average effect. Anything below 0.4 is a below-average effect. The art is working out why those influences with above-average effects differ from those influences with below-average effects. The

TABLE 1 Illustration of high and low impact effects on student achievement

INFLUENCE	ES	RANK	INFLUENCE	ES	RANK
Collective teacher efficacy	1.57	1	Class size	.21	193
Response to intervention	1.29	4	More finances	.21	196
Jigsaw method	1.20	7	Father's influence	.20	197
Developing self-efficacy	.92	11	Extracurricular programs	.20	198
Transfer Strategies	.86	14	Individualized programs	.19	199
Seeking help from peers	.83	15	Learning hierarchies	.19	200
Classroom discussion	.82	15	Co-/Team teaching	.19	201
Deliberate practice	.79	17	Within-class grouping	.18	202
Summarization	.79	18	One-on-one laptops	.16	206
Planning and prediction	.76	19	Ability grouping	.12	214
Repeated reading programs	.75	23	Teacher education	.12	216
Rehearsal and memorization	.73	26	Charter schools	.09	221
Feedback	.70	29	School calendars/ timetables	.09	222
Acceleration	.68	37	Single-sex schools	.08	225
Concept mapping	.64	40	Females vs. males	.08	227
Teachers not labeling students	.61	45	Whole language	.06	229
Direct instruction	.60	47	Student control over learning	0.2	234
Service learning	.58	56	Sleep	−.05	240
Practice testing	.54	70	Suspension of students	−.20	246
Second/third-chance programs	.53	72	Retention (hold back a year)	−.32	248

Note: ES = effect size.

answer is that the influences with above-average effects come down to how the teachers THINK. What makes the difference is *not* the structural issues that parents so often ask for (smaller class size, ability grouping, whether the school is charter or not) but the way the person leading the class or school thinks.

How great teachers think

The major finding from our research on teacher influences is that it is less *who* teachers are or *what* teachers do, and much more **how** they think – about their notion of impact, their expectations about their influence on students, and the evaluative decisions they make, moment by moment, in the class. Yes, it helps when teachers use high impact methods and interventions, but the most benefit comes when teachers, individually and collectively, have a 'high-impact mind frame'. Great teachers are teachers who collect evidence of their impact on all students. Great teachers then use this evidence to make the best decisions on what to do next in their teaching for optimal learning for students. We term this thinking 'evaluative thinking'.

We work in many thousands of schools across the world implementing the Visible Learning programs (see www.visiblelearning.com/ for more details). The top seven messages for teachers from our research are that, for optimal teaching and learning, teachers should do the following:

- Work together on evaluating their impact
- Identify what students bring to each lesson in terms of prior skills, wills (confidence, resilience), and thrills (motivations to learn)
- Be transparent from the outset about what success in the lessons look like (both about the content and ideas and about the relation between these ideas and transfer to new contexts)
- Make sure these success criteria meet the Goldilocks principle of not too hard, not too easy, and not too boring
- Ensure classrooms are inviting for students to learn, with a high-trust environment that allows students to see errors as opportunities for learning
- Seek evidence, all the time, from the students (their work, their assessments, their engagement) so they know the impact they have on student learning
- Focus relentlessly on the nature of learning and on teaching their students multiple strategies of learning

It is worthwhile not only to review what works best in schools but also to translate these messages to parents.

How great parents think

As with teachers, so it is for parents: It is less *who* parents are or *what* they do, but more *how* they think about their role, and how they think when making the moment-by-moment decisions that require judgment. It is about what they are aiming for, their high expectations, and their keenness to inspire the child to be involved in learning about their world. Similarly, it is about parents' understanding of what they want their impact to be and continually evaluating their impact on their children.

As you saw (in Chapter 4) it is less about being a particular type of parent, but about understanding how your child sees you as a parent. This means you need to be continually listening to your child to identify your impact – and this is one of the hardest parts of being a parent. It is not about the telling but about how the telling is understood – and how you understand how your messages are being received, understood, and actioned by your children.

The evidence about parenting

There are far fewer meta-studies on the effects of the home and parenting on children's learning than there are for teacher influences but enough to paint a picture that provides support for many of the arguments in this book.

The research on the effects of the home on student learning

There have been 59 meta-analyses relating to the effect of the home on student learning. Overall, the average effect of the home is low (an effect size of $d = 0.16$ is considered 'small'), and indeed your child's success at achievement after age 4 is very much dependent on the quality of the teachers and school – they have a much greater impact than the home.

However, first, although the home is less effective than we may think or want, this does NOT mean you can't make the home more influential. The ideal is for both school and home to enhance the child's learning, which is why we talk about parents investing in learning rather than being a substitute for the school teacher.

Second, many aspects of the home do not matter much. The least influence relates to whether the family is immigrant (indeed in

Australia, migrant children outscore local children, on average), on welfare, has parents who are employed or not, or the structure of the family. Love, caring, and high expectations are not reserved for the affluent.

Third, the greatest effects are the home environment, resources of the home (socioeconomic status), and expectations of parents. But be careful, postcode need not be a barrier. Note, for example, that the relationship between socioeconomic resources in the home are very low for measures of growth and improvement, but higher for achievement outcome measures. Indeed, there is some evidence that Australian teachers are among the world's best at adding value in schools for students from lower than from higher socioeconomic homes. Your child can bloom and grow in school independent of the home wealth. But when we relate home resources to achievement outcomes, then the higher socioeconomic status is privileged – but again care is needed as this could be part of the Matthew effect: Such children start ahead and stay ahead, with teachers and parents having higher expectations for those who start the year with higher levels of prior learning. If parents and teachers, however, have high expectations for all students, then postcode can be reduced in its power.

Table 2 provides the number of meta-analyses, the number of studies in these meta-studies, the number of effects, the average

TABLE 2 Summary of influences on achievement (from Visible Learning)

FAMILY INFLUENCES	NO. METAS	NO. STUDIES	NO. EFFECTS	ES	RANK (OUT OF 250)
Family resources and structure					
Socioeconomic status	7	622	1052	0.52	79
Welfare policies	1	8	8	−0.12	242
Family structure	4	231	576	0.16	205
Fathers	6	324	571	0.20	197
Divorced or remarried	8	395	441	0.23	182
Parental employment	2	88	1528	0.03	233
Adopted children	3	150	112	0.25	178
Immigrant status	1	53	74	0.01	236
Total/Average	32	1871	4362	0.16	194

FAMILY INFLUENCES	NO. METAS	NO. STUDIES	NO. EFFECTS	ES	RANK (OUT OF 250)
Family dynamics					
Home environment	3	48	122	0.52	78
Corporal punishment at home	1	16	16	−0.33	249
Television	3	37	540	−0.18	244
Parental involvement	15	883	2066	0.50	83
Parental autonomy support	3	258	251	0.15	208
Home visiting	2	71	52	0.29	164
Total/average	27	1313	3047	0.16	171
All parental influences	59	3184	7409	0.16	184

Note: ES = effect size.

effect size, and the ranking out of 250 (which includes influences from the home, school, curriculum, teaching). More detail is available at www.visiblelearningmetax.org).

Let's look at some of these in more detail.

Socioeconomic background

Socioeconomic status refers to the resources of the home, usually wealth and income. It is measured most often by the salaries of the parents, the income in the home, and proxies like the number of bathrooms, number of books in the home, and postcode. As commented above, it is more a measure of prior achievement, and has much lower relations to growth in school learning. Identical twins separated at birth into higher and lower socioeconomic families show that the explanation of different socioeconomic status is not great at all.

But there can be cultural differences between higher and lower socioeconomic households, and these often relate to the nature of expectations and encouragement about learning and schools. If you did not finish school, see much value in school, say, 'I can't do math', or didn't like school, then your children pick up these messages. If you say, 'I hated some of my teachers', then the messages are clear it is okay to hate some teachers. If you 'misbehaved' or condone misbehaviors at school, then do not be surprised that your children mimic you – you are the role models, the givers of permission to not like school! You have powerful effects on what your children aspire to and are encouraged to do and the investment they put into learning (both at school but also learning around the home). You are walking advertisements – so be aware of the messages your advertisements are sending to your children.

For many, high parental expectations about learning, and investment and confidence in the school system of teachers, have allowed them to be more employable, and gain higher resources as they moved into the workforce.

Better resourced parents may better game the system, as they are more likely to know the rules of schooling and are more often listened to by teachers and school leaders. This is often called the 'cultural capital' argument – but the parents with this capital are not always among the higher socioeconomic families.

Family structure

Does the nature of the family matter – divorced, foster, only child, gay parents? No. These effects from structural factors are small. Having fathers present can help, but often this is a bonus rather than a necessity, and the variability in effects among fathers is enormous (we return to this later). Similarly, divorce does not matter, although most effects of nondivorce are positive mainly because of the shared parenting and the extras provided by having other adults in the lives of students. Certainly, the tension in the home is more critical than whether there are one or two parents. Nor does it matter if the mother works or if the family has immigrant status or if the children are adopted.

The home environment

Features of the environment of the home can really matter. Allen Gottfried[1] identified the important influence of 'an intellectually more advantageous home'. He noted that this effect could be seen as early as 4 months, in terms of play materials, involvement in and variety of activities, and parent responsivity. However, it is also important to note that, in one of the first meta-studies, Barbara Iverson and Herb Walberg[2] found the effects of the home environment increased as the child became older.

Renee Strom and Franklin Boster[3] were interested in the home factors that possibly contributed to students dropping out before completing high school. Among the more compelling claims is whether the child feels they 'belong' in this place called school. This sense that your child 'belongs' in a learning environment is something you can influence. Belonging to a place of learning relates to the degree of support given by families and peers, and values and expectations are 'rooted in families and shared with family members'. Families with a permissive parenting style, low aspirations about schooling, and low levels of parent–child discussion increase the chances of children dropping out – regardless of the grades of students. On the other hand, for a student who is struggling with school, a home environment that supports 'belonging' can make a positive difference.

The average effect for positive communication about learning in the home on school completion was 0.44, and for communication in school, it was 0.28, while the greatest influence was shared parental expectations about school (0.65). This latter was identified by asking students about how far in school their parents expected them to go and the degree of communication conflict in the family. If students understand that school is important to their parents, this encourages the child to have a positive attitude toward school. Further, where a student feels negatively toward school, positive and supportive messages about schooling from parents may serve as a buffer against those negative feelings.[4]

Parental involvement

Being involved does not mean you should get involved with the school, volunteer in the lunchroom, or join the school board. The overall effects for this sort of involvement are low and are likely to decrease as the child moves through the grades, with minimal effects at high school. We have noted the low effects of homework, and when homework is subject to 'surveillance' by parents, the effects become negative (-0.30; see Chapter 7). Remember, homework is best when it is an opportunity to practice something the child has already learned. Making homework a negative experience reinforces to some students that school is no fun, not for them, and the work is not worthwhile. Some students do not know how to 'study' or learn without the teacher overseeing their engagement, so when they do not have such expertise in the home, homework is a grind. You can listen to them talk about their homework, help them practice conversations they can have with their teachers, show them how you can also struggle with homework, but never do it for them (John once completed a project for Kyle and failed – and has never been allowed to forget it).

In a comprehensive review of parental involvement, Charles Desforges and Alberto Abouchaar[5] concluded that discussions between parent and child about learning can have a significant positive effect on children's behavior and achievement even when the influence of background factors (e.g., social class, family size) has been factored out. In a comparison across 14 countries, Francesca Borgonovi and Guillermo Montt[6] investigated parental involvement and children's enjoyment of reading. In every country, to varying extents, parental involvement (even when factoring out socioeconomic home resources) made a difference – and they noted that '[m]any parent–child activities that are associated with better reading performance among students involve relatively little time and no specialized knowledge. What these activities do demand, though, is genuine interest and active engagement' (p. 50). Involvement included parents reading to children, discussing political or social issues with children, and the parents' own reading at home – at any age, young children to adolescence. Borgonovi and Montt concluded it is never too early or too late for parents to be involved with their children's reading.

We took part in the evaluation of the Flaxmere Project, a three-year set of interventions to engage parents in the learning of the children in five of the lowest socioeconomic schools in New Zealand.[ix] We found the major benefits came when homes started using the language of schooling. For example, one intervention provided computers in the homes: We found the real benefit came not from having computers in the home but from having people go into the homes to teach the families about the technology. These liaison people were former teachers, and it soon became apparent that it was not the learning about computers that had a positive effect but rather the language of learning coming into the home. The parents were learning how to talk to teachers, hearing teachers talk about learning, and listening to teachers in the act of teaching. As a result, the teachers noted improvements in the expectations of parents and children, more positive attitudes toward schooling and attendance, and greater interactions between parents and their children during the computer training. Children saw their parents learning alongside them, and the parents had a greater understanding of what their children were learning at school. Parents were more likely to go to the school on parent–teacher nights and interact with teachers. And the students' belief in their ability to engage and succeed at school was enhanced. We concluded:

> The success of the Flaxmere Project is primarily related to the success of finding ways for schools to 'invite' parents to learn more about their children's schooling, to learn more about the language of schools, and to collectively engage the community, parents, and caregivers of students in order to improve the current and long-term educational outcomes for students – in the home. So often parents are not as aware of what is required in today's schools, do not always have happy memories of their own school days, and thus are somewhat concerned about how best to help their children in succeeding in school. Given that the five Flaxmere schools are situated in one of the most poorly resourced home areas of New Zealand, for most parents the future success for their children is 'upwards' – for many through the hope of schooling. Without a doubt, the parents of Flaxmere children want the best for their children, have high expectations of schools as a place to assist their children, and wish to be involved in the most optimal ways to assist in their children's learning. Any image of an uncaring set of parents with low expectations and a carefree attitude should be well and truly put to rest in light of the evidence in this report. These parents rated their schools and their community as excellent, and had high expectations for the success of their schools to offer opportunities for their children to succeed.

Notes

1 Gottfried, A. W. (1984). Home environment and early cognitive development: Integration, meta-analyses, and conclusions. In *Home environment and early cognitive development: Longitudinal research* (pp. 329–342). Academic Press.

2 Iverson, B. K., & Walberg, H. J. (1980). Home environment. *Evaluation in Education*, 4, 107–108.

3 Strom, R. E., & Boster, F. J. (2007). Dropping out of high school: A meta-analysis assessing the effect of messages in the home and in school. *Communication Education*, 56(4), 433–452.

4 See Strom, R. E., & Boster, F. J. (2007). Dropping out of high school: A meta-analysis assessing the effect of messages in the home and in school. *Communication Education*, 56(4), 436–437.

5 Desforges, C., & Abouchaar, A. (2003). *The impact of parental involvement, parental support and family education on pupil achievement and adjustment: A literature review* (Vol. 433). DfES.

6 Borgonovi, F., & Montt, G. (2012). *Parental involvement in selected PISA countries and economies* (OECD Education Working Papers, No. 73). OECD Publishing. https://doi.org/10.1787/5k990rk0jsjj-en

Index

Note: Page numbers in *italics* indicate a figure and page numbers in **bold** indicate a table on the corresponding page.